Caring for the Scottish Home

Caring for the
Scottish Home

The National Trust
for Scotland

Royal
Commission on the
Ancient and
Historical
Monuments of
Scotland

Published by NMS Publishing Limited
National Museums of Scotland
Chambers Street
Edinburgh EH1 1JF

© The National Trust for Scotland and NMS Publishing Limited 2001

British Library Cataloguing in Publication Data
*A catalogue record of this book
is available from the British Library.*

ISBN 1 901663 57 4

Designed by Mark Blackadder.
In-house typesetting by Cara Shanley, NMS Publishing Limited.
Printed by Ebenezer Bayliss & Son Ltd, Worcester.

PHOTOGRAPHS ON PREVIOUS PAGES

Main picture: Roof shingles.
(BRUCE WALKER)
Above, right: Tenement House, Glasgow.
(NTS)
Below, right: Craobh Haven, Argyll.
(BENJAMIN TINDALL ARCHITECTS)

Acknowledgements

Ian M Davidson

I would like to thank all speakers participating in the conference of 2000 and
their willingness to allow their views to be published in this book. I owe a debt of
gratitude to those who have supported the development of these events in past
years, especially the lecturers from home and abroad and the delegates without
whom nothing could have happened.

The staff of the Grampian Region and latterly the North East Region have
been unswervingly helpful and supportive, and though it is invidious to single out
individuals I would like to mention my secretary, Irene Nimmo, and the Regional
Director David Sharland, without whose support little could have been achieved.
Mention should also go to Professor Charles McKean who was willing to offer help
and advice whenever it was needed.

Contents

This book, which helps celebrate ten years of the National Trust for Scotland's annual Building Conservation Conference, owes a debt of gratitude to the similarly titled *The Scottish Home*, edited by Annette Carruthers.

The National Trust for Scotland took a decision in 1990 to promote good conservation practice throughout Scotland, but particularly in the north. To this end the annual Building Conservation Conference was conceived. The initial event set the tone for future conferences. Many of the most informed lecturers, researchers and practitioners in the conservation of historic buildings were brought to Crathes Castle, near Aberdeen, for a two-day event that examined the technicalities of the conservative repair of stonework, woodwork, leadwork and so on. The conference was more successful than originally anticipated and this encouraged the Trust to organise an event each year thereafter, principally held in the north-east of Scotland.

Since 1990 the content of these events developed to include not only issues of technical concern but also the philosophical implications of such work on a building's sense of place and identity – indeed, no renovation work should be undertaken without a sound understanding of these implications. In latter years the conferences attempted to address this issue both at home and abroad. To this end we saw a significant international presence with speakers and representatives attending from the Estonian Heritage Society, the Society for the Protection of New England Antiquities, the York Civic Trust, Building Conservation International of Philadelphia, the National Trusts of Japan, and the authors of the Illustrated Burra Charter from Australia. Delegates have attended from all parts of the United Kingdom as well as from other countries.

In planning the conference for 2000 (and this book), the heritage considered was restricted to domestic structures, and no limit was placed on the extent to which these structures might be examined. The conference itself was designed to be wide and deep in its consideration of the issues, and the chapters selected for inclusion in this book are intended to be representative of it. They cover the rich architectural history of domestic buildings in Scotland; their development, form and function; the materials with which they were built; and the means by which they can be cared for. Gardens have not been forgotten, and their development alongside Scottish homes has also been included. Finally, an eye has been cast to how Scotland's homes might develop in the future. This book provides confirmation that care must always be judiciously applied to ensure the continuing survival of our rich heritage, both of the past and for the future.

Several of the chapters are the product of deep and intensive research undertaken by scholars at universities and national institutions. Others are the product of practical experience: the distilled knowledge of individuals, partnerships and companies. They all suggest the diversity of activity and opinion to be found. The homes referred to are from both the countryside and the town – each having their place in our cultural identity and each as worthy as the other, poor or rich, large or small. The actual buildings reflect the diversity of materials used

Craigievar Castle from the south. (NTS)

Preface

Ian M Davidson, *Conservation Manager – North East*
The National Trust for Scotland

throughout Scotland and highlight practical conservation within an examination of their place in the cultural heritage. Their authenticity resides not only in the stone and mortar, slate and plaster with which they are built, but also in their relationship with the environment, be it streetscape or wild landscape.

There is such a wide diversity of styles, materials and uses for homes throughout the regions of Scotland that it is difficult to identify them as clearly as one would wish to in a book like this. However, it is hoped that the evidence presented herein will act as a spur for others to carry out further research that will expand in detail on this variety.

Whenever possible the appropriate Scots word has been used to describe the item under consideration. Use has been made of the *Dictionary of Scottish Building* published in 1996. As with the materials and forms to be found throughout the

regions of Scotland, the words used to describe them are rich and varied. This presents an interesting dilemma for an editor. The most appropriate word has been used for the item under consideration given its context, and where a variety of terms could equally be applied the standard English description has been chosen.

We hope that the information and images in this book give a good idea of the variety of structures to be found in Scotland and the materials within them that have to be conserved. We hope that all those concerned and interested in the care of our homes and their future development will contribute to the ongoing study of Scotland's native architecture and the way it is used by the people who live in it. Many questions will be raised by the following chapters: they are intended to contribute to the discussion and to enrich and enliven the debate.

Fyvie Castle from the south.
(NTS)

It is a very great honour and privilege for me to introduce this book. I believe that we have much to celebrate in talking about *Caring for the Scottish Home*, and this publication has a special significance for the Trust.

I remember the Trust's first annual Building Conservation Conference taking place at Crathes Castle in 1990, though I was not present. It was very much an experiment at that time and attracted some 45 delegates, probably a good number in its day for an event that was relatively unusual. It was significant that it was held at Crathes, a building that had been much adapted over the years, including the complete rebuilding of the Queen Anne wing following a disastrous fire in the late 1960s. It thus provided a good setting for fertile discussion on the conservation of buildings of that nature, and particularly the way that they have been adapted over time. Whether we will be discussing the building in which we held the conference for 2000 (the Aberdeen Exhibition and Conference Centre) in the same way in 100 years' time I do not know, but it is an example of a building that well fulfils the function for which it was designed.

This book is special because it celebrates ten years of these events, during which time the original 45 delegates have grown to 140 in number. As well as lecturers and delegates from all over Scotland, they have come from a variety of places around the world, including Australia, Estonia, England, India, Japan and the United States of America. I believe that this signifies the importance of all our work in Scotland for conservation everywhere. This wide variety of people have brought very different experiences to enrich the knowledge and friendship of all those who have attended.

I was particularly interested that the title of the conference leading to this publication was 'Caring for the Scottish Home' rather than 'the Scottish House'. The event was extended specially to look beyond buildings and consider the much wider scope of the Trust's interests which make up the home – including gardens, collections, landscape, ecology and history, in addition to conservation of the buildings themselves. This reflects an increasingly holistic approach to the care of our properties which, I suggest, has changed significantly since 1990. Caring for the house, which forms the central core of the home, is not an exact science, and there will always be aspects of conservation work which, rightly, will be subject to debate and to changes of style and technique over the years. I am a geographer by background, and we are trained to assess a wide range of evidence and to draw conclusions from it. It has always been fascinating to me in the Trust to listen to differences of views, often between very eminent and highly respected people, and to try and reach my own judgement as to the correct way forward in a particular set of circumstances.

In encouraging such debate, the aim of the conferences is not only to promote the conservation of properties in the care of the Trust, but also to inform, educate and enthuse all those who attend on the best practice in caring for the nation's heritage. This caring is of course in the hands of many people – some in the charitable sector such as the Trust, some in the hands of Government and its

Gladstone's Land, Edinburgh.
(NTS)

Foreword

Trevor Croft, *Former Director, The National Trust for Scotland*

agencies, but most in the hands of private individuals or organisations. This wide range of interests is given prominence by the support for this conference from many organisations (including Historic Scotland, the Royal Commission on the Ancient and Historical Monuments of Scotland, and the Royal Incorporation of Chartered Surveyors in Scotland) whose sponsorship includes this prestigious publication.

This support emphasises the partnership that is now so important in so many aspects of our work. As the Trust's range of responsibilities increases, much cannot be achieved without the support of others. While finance is clearly vital in this regard, the sharing of skills and enthusiasm is equally important. In looking at the range of speakers at the tenth conference, some idea of the breadth of those skills became evident. I have had the pleasure of working with many of them and am unfailingly impressed by their enthusiasm and commitment to the task in hand. On those occasions, found in any job, when you feel that things are getting too much, their enthusiasm drives you forward with the view, 'I must do better!'

The Trust is unique amongst conservation organisations in Scotland in the range of its responsibilities in the conservation field. While this means we have great expertise in many areas, it also means that we can be thin on the ground and thus need to talk with and learn from others. Learning from others is nothing to be frightened about – rather the ability to do it and admit that we need to know more is a sign of strength. I believe that the Trust has an increasing willingness to engage with the wider community at home and abroad in promoting excellence in conservation with everyone involved, and it is certainly something I want to encourage. This can be done in part through lecturing, writing and discussion, but it must never be a one-way process. As part of this the Trust must listen to constructive criticism and engage freely in the wider debate with an open mind, willing to learn where necessary and equally to be constructive in its support and engagement with others.

It is this bringing together which I believe makes the conferences and this book so special and justifies the Trust's efforts since 1990, as well as the help which has come from all our supporters.

Charlotte Square, north side, Edinburgh. Home of the National Trust for Scotland until 2000 when the Head Office moved to the south side of the Square. These buildings are now home to the Edinburgh World Heritage Site Offices. (NTS)

This publication marks the tenth conference in the admirable series organised by the National Trust for Scotland. Its subject – 'Caring for the Scottish Home' – was rather less specific than some of its predecessors. The expertise displayed in the following chapters creates a problem for the opening author as he struggles neither to steal their thunder, which in reality is not very likely, nor to reveal his ignorance, which is.

'Caring' has become a fashionable word and seems now to be used more in a social context than a practical one. In modern terminology it could be described as 'PC' (politically correct) and is seldom used to describe things like sweeping the leaves or cleaning the gutters, even if the latter are 'PVC' (politically very correct). The word 'care', rather surprisingly, has nothing to do with the Latin *cura*, but is Teutonic in origin. In its earliest recorded sense it means 'trouble' or 'grief', even 'sickness': Burns uses it in this sense in *The Banks o' Doon*, where he describes himself as being 'sae weary fu' o' care'. It can also, however, be a transitive verb, and its use thus (although archaic) is most expressive – as in 'I'm going to spend the weekend caring my house'. If everybody did that, this publication would not be necessary.

Like 'care', the word 'home' has many meaningful associations and evocative overtones. We are familiar with the saying that 'an Englishman's home is his castle'. The rest of the world is, of course, convinced that all Scotsmen live in castles anyway, but is the corollary true – that a Scotsman's castle is his home? Does 'home' have the same symbolic meaning for the owner of a Highland keep as it does for the occupant of a house in Golden Square or a tenement flat in Govan?

One all too typical Scottish approach (although, as you will realise, it may have Greek origins) was brought home to me many years ago when watching a play at the old Gateway Theatre in Edinburgh. Euripides, the Greek dramatist, makes his character Electra say, 'Tis joy to him that toils when toil is o'er to find home waiting, full of happy things'. There was not much that was happy in poor Electra's life and I'm glad for her that she had a nice place to come home to where she could, shall we say, 'bury the hatchet'. The concept of home as a significant aspect of the physical and moral life of human beings is probably as old as life itself. In the lares and penates of the Romans, the status of the home was raised to that of the minor deities and was publicly worshipped. It was Pliny who first said, 'Home is where the heart is', and even the great Dr Samuel Johnson who (providing he was not speaking about Scotland) usually made a great deal of sense, said in *The Rambler*, 'To be happy in the home is the ultimate result of all ambition'.

The adjectives we associate with the word 'home' have heavily subjective overtones – 'family home', 'childhood home', 'broken home' – and the word has been purloined to give respectability to its exact opposite. I once heard a mother threatening her child, saying, 'If you don't behave yourself, I'll put you in a home'. We use 'home' as an adjective as well – 'the home country', 'the home team', 'home rule'. Some of you may be old enough to recall the embarrassment caused to the Scottish National Party when the Earl of Home became Prime Minister and the

Castle Fraser.
(NTS)

Caring for the Scottish Home

Sir James Dunbar Nasmith, *Consultant Architect*
Law & Dunbar Nasmith, Architects

signs that were plastered all over Scotland saying 'Home Rule for Scotland' had to be removed.

'Home' comes from Old English 'ham' and is generally associated with things small and intimate, and therefore the concept of caring for it has overtones of personal involvement. What is not in the philology, however, but is implicit in the way we use the word (and certainly, for me, in the title of the tenth conference and this book), is the element of love and self-sacrifice that caring for anything entails. Indeed, to say that you 'care for' someone means that you love them. Throughout the ages people have loved and cared for their homes in a very special way – it can be an obsession, even a form of madness; but the desire to do so is deeply rooted in our psyche and is a major factor that moulds our society. Most people believe it to be a force for good and we should pay tribute to the generations before us who treasured their homes so much that they devoted themselves to ensuring their survival – often sacrificing their livelihood, and sometimes even their lives. These homes are now our heritage, and had they not been so cherished they would not exist today.

Why, therefore, does a particular assemblage of building materials inspire such unique devotion when similar assemblagies, possibly even in the same street, inspire nothing? A great deal of research has been done on the subject and I am indebted to my friend and erstwhile colleague, the environmental psychologist Professor Peter Aspinall, for giving me information about it. A collection of papers assembled by Alltman and Low entitled *Place Attachment* is particularly relevant but, if I am honest, it does little more than confirm what one knows instinctively – namely that people feel a strong attachment to what they think of as home. The research methods used to establish this generally accepted phenomenon to the satisfaction of the researcher are unintelligible to anyone who is not trained in the science and techniques of the subject. Rudyard Kipling, whom I suspect did not do a five-year research programme to justify his statement, wrote:

> *God gives all men all earth to love,*
> *But, since man's heart is small*
> *Ordains for each one spot shall prove*
> *Belovèd over all.*

Most of us, I submit, would agree with him, and for many of us the one spot to which he refers will be home. There is a technique called 'eco-analysis' that provides a method of exploring individual experience of places, in a way that is relevant to making design decisions about them and that makes the core identity of those places explicit. Its purpose is similar to that of conservation plans (with which most readers will be familiar) which, by means of painstaking research and analysis, establish the cultural significance of a place. It will be agreed, however, that such plans may establish the most significant qualities of a place without explaining to us how we make the value judgements that cause us to accept some aspects and to reject others. So far as homes are concerned it will, I think, also be agreed that the attraction of the home is not only a particular property of the building, but a consonance between the owner and the building that depends just as much on the emotions and desires of the owner, as it does on any intrinsic quality which the building may possess. Some people appear to have no nesting instinct and the concept of home has very little, if any, significance for them. Others are passionately

Crathes Castle ceiling repair in the 1960s.
(NTS)

attached to their home environment and any desecration to, destruction of or removal from this beloved domain can cause severe psychological disturbance, the symptoms of which are well known in psychiatric medicine.

The philosopher Immanuel Kant wrote, 'All our consciousness is grounded in spatial experience'. He was referring not only to the emotional ties that the concept of home places on us, but also to the fact that the very ground of our being is bound up to our relationship with the space around us. It is a concept that takes an effort to get your mind around, but even using the phrase 'getting your mind round something' suggests that he may be right. It is impossible to divorce one's experience (memory) from the environment in which that experience took place. Those memories are part and parcel of the emotions, which may have included feelings of love, of hate, or of indifference. Indeed, the same environment and upbringing may have caused contradictory emotions in members of the same family who appear to have been exposed to identical conditions, so that the congruence of a place with one person is unlikely to coincide with that of another. It is the sum of these individual congruences that creates the collective consciousness which is so important in formulating our attitudes towards our environment. And it is our attitude towards our environment that preserves or destroys our heritage.

Corstorphine, Edinburgh.
Late 17th-century house, photographed *circa* 1900.
(SCOTTISH LIFE ARCHIVE, NMS)

So far, I have been talking about the effect of this attachment to the home on individuals, but what is true of individuals is also true of nations. It was Walter Scott who said:

> *Breathes there the man, with soul so dead,*
> *Who never to himself hath said,*
> *This is my own, my native land!*

All of us, particularly if we are Scottish, are conscious of such sentiments, and most of us can probably identify particular moments or experiences when pride in our country brought tears to our eyes. The occasions may be embarrassingly sentimental – perhaps the lone piper at the Tattoo, or that nightly image of Eilean Donan Castle being pursued by a hot-air balloon or, more seriously, a sudden image of particular and unexpected beauty – like the north side of the Old Town of Edinburgh bathed in evening sunshine, or snow sparkling on a Perthshire hill. These are images, quite literally, 'to die for'. I use that rather trite and fashionable phrase deliberately because when people went off to war 'to die for their country' they needed an image of that kind to reassure them they were not dying in vain. The emotional bond which linked them to their home was subsumed by a similar bond linking them to their country, and that subsumption was grounded more firmly in 'place' than in abstract concepts like freedom or democracy. We lose such bonds at our psychological peril. In cherishing them, we cherish what makes for a stable and caring society. In caring for our homes, we care for Scotland.

This chapter is about understanding. We are beset by myths in Scotland – myths in which architecture so often plays a prominent role (of a warlike people still living in primitive castles during the Renaissance, for example) – that obscure or inhibit that understanding. The Scottish home may represent social history in stone, but it is a history often in ruins and customarily mis-interpreted. A reconsideration of what was built, and why, is long overdue.

Richard Emerson, Chief Inspector of Historic Buildings, focuses upon the town house, and Simon Green, of the Royal Commission on the Ancient and Historical Monuments of Scotland, upon the rural dwelling. (Note the difference in terminology.) Emerson's focus is upon what makes the Scottish town house different from those of our neighbours, attributing it to Scotland's peculiar political and ecclesiastical circumstances. These conferred upon the town house the important role of burghal status symbol. Briefly tracing the history of the town house from aristocratic *hôtel* to the terrace, be it of town houses or of tenements, he suggests that Scottish builders and architects created an unusual urban grandeur in a country in which the usual urban patrons were conspicuous by their absence. Simon Green then considers the nature of village and rural architecture, the forces that shaped it, its adaptability for the present, and its cultural implications. Robin Turner, Archaeologist to the National Trust for Scotland, expounds how the archaeologist's input has made a significant contribution to Trust work and presentation. Finally, Charles McKean, Professor of Scottish Architectural History at the University of Dundee, suggests a methodology for use in decoding building history as the first step to under-standing how Scottish homes changed and adapted over time.

The Development of Scottish Domestic Architecture in Cities, Towns and Villages

Richard Emerson

Towns are one of the things that we do best in Scotland, and town planning is a particularly Scottish virtue – of which Patrick Geddes was a product rather than a harbinger. It is the planned towns like Thurso, Keith, Findochty and Inveraray that stick in the memory. But Inveraray also illustrates how some of our finest town houses are no longer in towns. Inveraray, Tyninghame, Gordon Castle and Cullen House all demonstrate the consequences of removing the town some distance away from the big house. The town house of Menzies of Pitfodels in the heart of Fordyce, therefore, is a rare example of what was once commonplace: towers and nobleman's Renaissance houses enmeshed in the fabric of the town. At the smaller end was the 'baronial hall' in Gorbals High Street (now demolished), and on a royal scale, Holyrood and Linlithgow.

Glasgow tenement.
(NTS)

The Development of Scotland's Domestic Buildings

Editor: Professor Charles McKean

The decamping of the aristocracy from the town, and of the Royal Family from Scotland in 1603, deprived us of an element that many continental towns still rely upon – the local aristocrat's palace. Argyle's Lodging in Stirling, extended by Sir Anthony Alexander in 1632 in anticipation of Charles II's visit in the following year, shows the effect that the seventeenth-century equivalent of a royal walkabout and photo opportunity could have in galvanising client and architect alike to superior endeavours. Furthermore, Sir William Bruce's Kinross House and Dunkeld House both demonstrate that having a town on your doorstep, even at the end of the seventeenth century, was considered no embarrassment.

The presence of a Parliament could inspire palaces, of which Queensberry House was the finest and largest. However, its fate – of being converted to a barracks in 1820 – is typical, given that the Hanoverian army had taken over the royal palaces at Stirling and Edinburgh, and burnt Linlithgow. Lauderdale House in Dunbar was a rare post-Union example of a noble house in the heart of the burgh, but its increasingly unfashionable situation condemned it, too, to conversion to barracks. Otherwise, post-Union town houses for the aristocracy were generally smaller, like Milton House by William Adam, an influential villa whose descendants still people our late Georgian suburbs.

If our political history meant that our towns had, thereafter, to do without the mansions of the nobility, our ecclesiastical history also deprived us of numerous bishop's palaces. Is a manse a substitute for a palace at St Andrews, Aberdeen, Brechin, Dunblane, Dunkeld, Elgin, Fortrose, Lismore and Whithorn? The two bishop's palaces that do survive, one ruined at Kirkwall, and the other still roofed at Dornoch (now the Castle Hotel), retain the power to surprise.

Another aspect of what has been lost from Scottish burghs is their original materials. Early nineteenth-century Jedburgh's buildings were mostly roofed in thatch.[1] Auchtermuchty had much thatch still remaining 30 years ago, and planned towns like Cuminestown in Aberdeenshire were, until recently, hiding thatch under corrugated iron roofs. Crovie, the very model of a fisher town with corrugated iron roofs giving way to pantiles as gentrification proceeded, was slated in the eighteenth century with the coarse greywacke slates from Melrose, only a mile or two away, the qualities of which are praised in the *First Statistical Account*.[2] Materials also change with fashion. No one these days likes the bull-faced imitation rubble once so characteristic of many parts of Scotland, and villages like Eyemouth and Lauder now present a more conventionally attractive face than they did 20 years ago. Harl, thick and white with lumps like a school pudding, has unified vernacular architecture across the country, displacing smooth stone-coloured render lined as ashlar, slaister-pointing, sneck-harling and a myriad of nameless local building traditions. It may have done more. The National Galleries of Scotland's exhibition 'Designs of Desire'[3] contains a number of designs for painted architecture – fictive ornament on the outside of town houses. They are all foreign, of course, and on the Continent the tradition survives. It thrived once in Scotland – painted external architecture can be dimly discerned on the Chapel Royal in Stirling, while the fictive ribs of the vault spanning the front of Craigston, Aberdeenshire, are still very clear. External painting survived into the nineteenth century even in small towns like Tranent, with houses immaculately painted with rusticated ashlar blocks; while many a classical house and New Town house can provide examples of painted fanlights and painted dummy windows. Who knows what we lost in our rubble-mania when it was all stripped off?[4]

Rubble-mania also blinded us to the potential of plaster. Eighteenth-century

Scotsmen who admired the exuberance achieved on the Continent brought over central European *stuccadores* like Joseph Enzer to decorate the insides of their houses (like the House of Dun, Angus) in exactly this way. But was it just the insides? Only a few miles from Dun, the Old House of Hedderwick has not only key blocked and egg-and-dart moulded architraves, but an ornate plaster Father Time, large as life, scythe and all, floating on the front of the facade of what is but a minor laird's house. Behind him you can see good familiar rubble, as insistently the cultivar returns to native stock. Had the Royal Commission not recorded this, who would have been able to show from the rubble walls, a decade later, that this tradition had taken root in Scotland – and who, confronted by this example, can say with confidence that it took root only once?

Envisage, therefore, a town of houses, not white rendered and red tiled like Salazar's Portugal but, like Portugal pre-Salazar, stone-coloured (with stone, stucco and painted architecture)[5] and not a bit of rubble in sight, thatched around the edges and slated at its centre. We also once had our own arcaded Plaza Majors, Places Royales and Covent Gardens. We built arcades along our broad market streets and, lest anyone should miss the point, called them 'piazzas'. Elgin and Inverness, as well as Edinburgh, constructed their big continental squares by relying not on kings to ordain their great civic improvement, but on an effort of collective will. Individual citizens in their town house or tenement block were to build the piazzas incrementally – save in Glasgow where, after the 1652 fire, it was a Council requirement.[6] The extent to which these efforts of collective will succeeded cannot now be judged, but the surviving examples at Elgin, dated 1688 and 1694, were sufficiently remarkable to be criticised by Dr Johnson as being of no great use as shelters from the rain, and conducive to people loitering out of doors when they should be more usefully occupied.[7] The tenement with an arcaded ground floor was still being built in neo-classical Union Street, Aberdeen, in the early nineteenth century, and an arcade now defines the southern perimeter of Edinburgh's Parliament Square since its rebuilding in smart classical guise after the 1824 fire.

It is this collective effort – collective vision and collective will – that is the defining characteristic of the Scottish burghs. Anyone who has lived in a planned town in the north-east will know how determined and unforgiving is this unity or conformity of view. If insularity (or even narrow-mindedness) is the downside, it is the glueing together of individual house or tenement units that lends grandeur and monumentality to our burghs. Medieval Perth ringed itself with modern Georgian terraces by Robert Reid on the South Inch, anticipating his Great King Street in Edinburgh's New Town by five years. William Burn was brought in to create Bridge of Earn,[8] intending a pair of terraces confronting each other at the southern end of Rennie's new bridge, of which only one was built. The bridge itself is Adam Smith made adamantine, and the New Town the first evidence of the economic improvement it embodies. At Dunkeld the same drama is played out on a bigger scale at the end of Telford's new bridge, with initial proposals again by Reid.[9]

The upside is evident in the determination with which Edinburgh sustained its ambitions for a classical New Town through almost a century, completing Gillespie Graham and Playfair's great neo-classical set pieces after their death, the cold hail of Ruskin's scorn stinging in their faces:

> *Walk around your Edinburgh buildings and look at the height of your eye,*
> *what will you get from them? Nothing but square-cut stone – square-cut*

The exuberant plasterwork by Joseph Enzer at the House of Dun, Angus. (NTS)

stone – a wilderness of square-cut stone for ever and ever: so that your houses look like prisons, and truly are so; for the worst feature of Greek architecture is, indeed, not its costliness but its tyranny.[10]

It is not possible to be certain whether this fierce sense of community values, of common effort leading to common good, is a consequence of tenement living or makes tenement living possible, but in tracing the history of the town house the tenement bulks large. We have a few late-medieval town houses, but early survivors facing marketplaces or High Streets are likely to be tenements – like Gladstone's Land, Mowbray House and John Knox's house, all facing Edinburgh's High Street, and Gardyne's Land facing Dundee's. Even the grandest houses – Mars Wark, Stirling, and Moray House, Edinburgh – had shops on the ground floor, and the form proved unstoppable: see Robert Adam's unsuccessful proposal for South Bridge, Edinburgh.[11] South Bridge as built by Robert Kay has two levels of shops, one facing South Bridge and one Niddrie Street, below and behind, with houses above. At its most multi-layered, on the corner of North St Andrew Street and York Place, there are four floors of shops with houses above. This is more than a corner – it is a turning point. The road now divides with great tenemental canyons of housing over shops in one direction and multi-storey shopping, the housing squeezed out, in the other.

Rows of such tenements glued together, standing shoulder to shoulder as in Haddington, are what makes the town. Who instantly remembers its medieval colle-

Walter Geikie (1795-1837), *Lawn market from above the West Bow.* (NMS LIBRARY)

giate church? Where is it in the townscape? The grand urban statement of Aberdeen's 1801 proposal for Union Street is made up of no more than tenements and shops. What here is the city but its people? Similarly, the ancestor of the terraced town house is found in Tobias Bauchop's House in Alloa, a home all in polished ashlar and polished classicism (by Sir William Bruce for his builder?). It is the glueing together of such houses in rows that creates a town's character as in, say, Kirkcudbright.

Control freaks (planners, provosts, surveyors and architects are control freaks) soon realised that those houses could be more strictly marshalled into crescents or squares, and individuality suppressed. All the houses in Atholl Crescent, Edinburgh, for example, are the same, and none is rectangular. Such urban megalomania reached its peak with the great neo-classical wall of St Bernard's Crescent in Edinburgh. It is not immediately obvious that it contains houses. Most of them have no individual garden, Dean Street is immediately behind, and some barely have a view to the front, blinkered as they are by giant order columns. Yet these houses must have been among the most expensive in Edinburgh to build.

There was fierce competition between the developers of the rival New Town streets, so what compelled people to spend their money on this inhabited wall rather than a nice house with a garden and a view? It can only have been their wish to buy into the vision, the 'dream of great genius' as Benjamin Haydon called it[12] – a creation of ordinary people exercising their will. When the First Minister and his Cabinet sit in state in Bute House, they are the successors not to some duke or earl but to the shoemaker who built the grandest house in Charlotte Square in 1798.

Charlotte Square, Edinburgh.
(NTS)

In combining to present a unified face to the world, builders, owners, architects, surveyors, tenants, citizens and councillors gave monumental urban grandeur to a land in which the usual urban players were conspicuous by their absence.

Ardmor on the southern fringe of Cockle Shore, Barra.
(SCOTTISH LIFE ARCHIVE, NMS)

Glamis Estate workers' cottages, now the Angus Folk Museum.
(NTS)

In the following section, Simon Green casts a similarly appraising eye over the nature and culture of the rural buildings of Scotland.

Buildings of the Scottish Countryside

Simon Green

The Buildings of the Scottish Countryside by Robert J Naismith is the product of large-scale systematic fieldwork commissioned in 1979 by the Countryside Commission for Scotland.[1] This informative book covers the period from 1750 to 1914, when Scotland was at its wealthiest, and its buildings most polite and easy on the eye. It examines in detail the building types and myriad of regional variations that make up our unique built heritage, and provides a blueprint of the character of traditional buildings in the countryside. The field records of the survey and the resulting data are available in the National Monuments Record of Scotland at the Royal Commission on the Ancient and Historical Monuments of Scotland (RCAHMS).[2] Later studies, including that by John and Margaret Richards,[3] have used it as a sourcebook for guidelines on how to introduce new buildings into the countryside. The RCAHMS has been recording farm buildings for many years, now under the auspices of the Farm Buildings Survey. With the assistance of Susannah Wade Martins and Dr John Shaw, the Survey is undertaking detailed systematic surveys of farms of different types throughout Scotland. The various conferences and invaluable field trips of the Scottish Vernacular Buildings Working Group have greatly increased our knowledge, complementing the fascinating ethnographic researches of the School of Scottish Studies.[4]

Early human settlement has left many traces on our countryside. Climate change has meant that areas which were once cultivated and inhabited are now abandoned. Land use patterns have all left their mark. The RCAHMS survey of settlement at Achiltibuie in Wester Ross, entitled *Achiltibuie – the Archaeology of a Crofting Landscape*,[5] provides a good illustration of how a landscape has been changed through man's buildings and farming methods. The earliest evidence for occupation comes from three Bronze Age burials found along the coast at Achiltibuie, Rubh'a'Mhadaidh and Reiff, while the first recorded settlements – hut circles probably dating to the first millennium BC – are located on either sides of Lochs Vatachan and Raa. The hut circles and their field systems lie on ground abandoned to moorland in the mid first millennium BC, when cooler and wetter climatic conditions set in. By the later Iron Age (300 BC–AD 300), the only settlements known are a broch at Achiltibuie and a dun at Achnahaird, both of which lie on the coast. Although two medieval buildings have been found at Achnahaird, there is no documentary evidence of settlements in the area before 1550. Blaeu's map of 1654 shows that several of the pre-crofting settlements had earlier origins.

The footings of these buildings, round-ended and smaller than both the eighteenth/nineteenth-century houses and medieval buildings at Achnahaird, survive. In the early nineteenth century the Cromarty Estate created a series of crofting townships and turned large areas of pasture over to sheep-runs. By 1850 all the earlier townships, except Badentarbat, had been converted to crofts. The number of crofts and the population has declined throughout the twentieth century.

Areas that some regard as wilderness contain numerous traces of development, as the survey carried out by the RCAHMS at the Mar Lodge Estate in 1996 (Mar Lodge Estate, *Grampian: An Archaeological Survey*) confirms.[6] The Mar Lodge Estate has been a hunting forest since the Middle Ages, when it was owned by the Earls of Mar, but for most of its history there was permanent settlement along the valley of the Dee. Constrained by mountainous terrain and the need to preserve the pine-woods and hunting grounds, it did not spread further up. In summer, some tenants moved their cattle and sheep to the upland shielings and, by the early eighteenth century, many of the shielings in Glens Lui and Ey had become permanent farms. This proved to be a short-lived phase, ending in the late eighteenth century when the Earl of Fife cleared many of the farms and turned large areas into sheep-runs. These in turn were cleared in order to create what was known as the New Forest of Mar on the south of the Dee, which was again adapted to create the great Edwardian shooting estate that is now in the ownership of the National Trust for Scotland.

The old and the new on Barra.
(SCOTTISH LIFE ARCHIVE, NMS)

The improvement and mechanisation of farming techniques through the eighteenth and nineteenth centuries produced a wonderful array of purpose-built buildings. Almost every estate had its model farm, like that at Aden in Banffshire or Maam in Argyll on the Duke of Argyll's estate. As areas were drained and cultivated, earlier settlements cleared and new buildings erected, the look of the countryside changed dramatically. Certainly the most famous of such initiatives were the improvements of the Sutherland Estate, which constructed a series of highly mechanised farms like that at Clynelish in 1871. The Balfour family on Shapinsey in Orkney improved the entire island, complete with state-of-the-art steading and mill, as well as a substantial country house to the designs of David Bryce.[7]

The Red House, Mar Lodge Estate.
(NTS)

Up until the mid nineteenth century, most buildings in the countryside were built in traditional ways with local materials using tried and tested techniques. Thereafter, a combination of the advent of the railways, the development of the shooting estate, and the rise of the architectural profession, made the story much more complicated. Railways supplied the tin sheeting that adorns so many of our most picturesque cottages – so much so that it is now regarded as a vernacular material, even though it is hardly indigenous. Concrete was also used for farms and estate buildings as soon as it was available; it was used, for example, on the Ardtornish Estate, Ardnamurchan, in the 1870s. Although our traditional methods of building are of vital importance, and lime – and its use – will be of prime importance for the future of our built environment, whether in the countryside or not, our predecessors welcomed new materials and we should not ignore them. Nor should we avoid using traditional materials and methods in new ways. Otherwise we shall end up killing our growing and changing traditions; simply curating a nationwide museum of building. The buildings of the Scottish countryside are of vital importance to the nation, but they must adapt and change – as they always have done – or else we become a sterile nation, trapped in a 'Grannie's Hieland Hame' tourist theme park.

The importance of farm buildings, especially the improved farm complex with cart house, byre, granary and horse gang, to the character and history of rural Scotland has been underestimated. Authentic examples are becoming increasingly rare with the vogue for 'barn' conversions and the introduction of Velux windows. The thatched cottage, almost a national symbol, cannot be maintained totally successfully without the traditional lifestyle, as the weaving of symonds to support the thatch roofs of Orkney illustrates.[8]

The necessarily large modern barns, silos and silage clamps are rarely items of beauty, and good modern design should be encouraged for them as it was 200 years ago. If we wish to preserve our traditional farm buildings, it is really up to the National Trust for Scotland, or some other organisation, to subsidise farmers to maintain them in perpetuity, as is being done in the English Lake District. Or should there be a Redundant Farm Buildings Trust? The danger is that once a farm building is not used for the processes for which it was designed, it loses so much; yet the scale of modern agricultural machinery is incompatible with that of farms only decades old, never mind centuries old. That remains the problem.

In the next section, Robin Turner examines how the archaeological process can enrich our knowledge and understanding of historic structures and lifestyles.

Appearances can be Deceptive

Robin Turner

The application of 'buildings archaeology' has been relatively slow in coming to Scotland, but archaeologists are increasingly included in projects involving the conservation or alteration of historic buildings. Trying to unravel the history of a building without the assistance of systematic drawn and written records is like investigating the scene of a crime without bringing in forensic scientists. The principal clues might be found by other means, but they are just as likely to be overlooked or misinterpreted. Archaeologists are now habitually called in by the National Trust for Scotland at an early stage of any initiative which involves changes to a historic building or structure, and the application of archaeological techniques is proving revealing – as can be demonstrated by a few examples.

The Trust's oldest formerly inhabited structure is a crude shelter, primarily made of turf, recently discovered over 2000ft up Ben Lawers. It is dated by radio-carbon dating to 7000 BC, placing it in the earliest Mesolithic period.[1] Like most Scottish buildings over the following 8500 years, the Ben Lawers structure was made of readily available local materials – easy to collect and, unfortunately from an archaeologist's perspective, easy to re-use. Although there are examples of later prehistoric and early historic vernacular structures, the persistent use of turf, stone, timber and thatch has meant the constant recycling of building materials in the countryside until relatively recent times.

Archaeological techniques are being used to examine how people lived in sites inhabited during the last 200 years. Excavations in the later 1980s on Hirta, for example, helped reveal the truth about the inhabitants of St Kilda in the last few decades before the evacuation in 1930. The islanders would have us believe they eked a primitive living from the meagre natural resources of the islands, but their material culture tells a very different story.[2] Imported goods from far and wide show that the St Kildans enjoyed a relatively sophisticated lifestyle, to some extent playing to the cameras when the tourists came to be amazed and amused. The remains of leather shoes and other items of clothing show us that early twentieth-century St Kildans dressed much the same as their neighbours in the Western and Northern Isles. They enjoyed some of the finer things in life – luxuries including Camp Coffee and Parisian clothing accessories – and there was much less reliance on traditional activities such as egg collecting and fowling than commonly thought. From 1860 they lived in the latest modern accommodation that became cosier as the nineteenth century progressed, and their activities became increasingly tourist-orientated from 1877 onwards. It is sobering to think that the St Kildans had reached such a level of reliance on tourism that they ultimately lost the way of life that had enabled them to enjoy a sustainable lifestyle for centuries, if not millennia. The balance of sustainable development had tipped too far by the 1920s and the whole social and economic system became unviable[3] – a lesson, surely, for the fragile rural environment of Scotland today.

Perhaps the Trust was carrying on this tradition of giving people what they expected, rather than relying on reality, when it took the decision in the 1930s to alter a newly-acquired blackhouse at Callanish: the building was simply not 'typical enough'. Trust records show that alterations were made to the plan of the building, following local advice, in order to make it more representative of its type. Nowadays we place greater emphasis upon authenticity. Following a careful archaeological survey of the site, undertaken with the assistance of local volunteers, we have a better understanding of the development – particularly the recent development – of the house.[4] Its key significance may be not as an authentic Highland Scottish home, but as an insight into the philosophy of conservation and the idea of the 'Scotch Hame' between the wars.

Detailed archaeological surveys sometimes reveal buildings to have been

Above: St Kilda, the village street.
(NTS)

Left: Loch Tay, Ben Lawers area, early Mesolithic in date.
(NTS)

Old Auchentroig, recently conserved by the Trust under its Little Houses Improvement Scheme following archaeological investigations.
(NTS)

much more significant than had previously been believed. An analysis of the fabric of the bothy at Canna Harbour – a part-demolished three-bay structure with the outward appearance of a string of ordinary harbourside cottages – confirmed grander origins.[5] Lieutenant Pierce's watercolour of the harbour in 1787 shows Coroghon House in this location (an imposing three-storey central pile with single-storey bays on either side) before it was superseded in the 1860s by the present Canna House.[6] The central part of the bothy buildings requiring extensive roof repairs in 1997, a detailed archaeological survey was undertaken,[7] including a plan and a measured drawing of each elevation. These illustrated and described each different element of the building, from a window or door to a structural crack or blocked opening. This enabled a representation of the building to be compared with the eighteenth-century watercolour, revealing an exact match between the pattern of original door and window openings and the three-storey central section of Coroghon House. The archaeological survey also served as a record of the building before it was conserved, and helped in making subsequent conservation decisions.

King's Stables Cottage at Culloden, although a Scheduled Ancient Monument because of its association with the battle, had clearly been considerably altered in the past. It was even suggested that it might have been entirely fabricated in imitation of Old Leanach Cottage that lies on the battlefield, now used by the Trust for interpretation. The possibility of de-scheduling was even considered. After undertaking their survey, archaeologists concluded that much more of King's Stables Cottage was authentic than had been thought[8] – indeed, it might be more intact than Old Leanach Cottage.

A garden building which said a lot about the people who lived in the 'big house' was the vinery. In 1948, the one at Culzean was in such a dilapidated state that it had to be taken down, leaving little more than an ugly cement-rendered wall with a simple flower bed in front. As one of the last projects of the Culzean Stonework Appeal, the vinery (now known as the Fruit Range) is to be recreated, necessitating an archaeological assessment of the standing and buried remains. Although it was clear that the heated rear wall, with its integral flue system to carry hot air, was largely intact, the condition of the below-ground deposits was unknown. An archaeological assessment by Trust staff revealed the remains of the second main phase of the vinery, dating to the first half of the nineteenth century. Fieldwork uncovered a remarkable system of elaborate hot air drains beneath the soil which would have kept the sensitive vine roots free of frost. Deposits of charcoal and crushed lime mortar relate to the conditioning of the soil to enhance vine growth, and the presence of large concentrations of horse bones tallies with contemporary gardening documents describing how best to establish new plants. The Culzean vinery demonstrates the lengths people were prepared to go to in order to propagate the status symbol of year-round grapes. Similar arrangements will have been devised at the many other vineries in Scotland, but few now survive since the evidence is vulnerable to being swept away for new uses. Once consolidated, the excavations are to form part of the interpretation of the new building, and the building design has been modified so as to minimise disturbance to the remaining buried deposits (see also Bob Heath's comments on Culzean, page 51).

Architectural history, like archaeology, is fundamentally about understanding our ancestors' culture, how they lived and how their ideas developed. Both disciplines depend upon the careful study of building design and construction. The Trust's Longhouse at Moirlanich, near Killin, one of the first vernacular buildings to be recorded for the Trust in particular detail, provided evidence from throughout its 200-year development. Twentieth-century artefacts from the loft and the dried-out compost in the byre at Moirlanich were all saved, and earlier material was found in a small adjacent walled vegetable plot (transported there from the byre during manuring in the nineteenth century). One of the most interesting observations came during an (unsuccessful) attempt to obtain a tree-ring date for some of the timbers. An analysis of the species used revealed a notable collection of types: ash or elm for the cruck blades; pine for the collars; and pine for the purlins. The immediate assumption was that the house builders had simply used whatever timber was locally available, but further investigation of historical sources for the area indicated that different wood was chosen for different functions in house building. This small observation provides insight into the choices made by the builders of the longhouse. They did not grab what they could get from as near as they could, but obtained what was best for the purpose.[9]

A number of rare survivals help to retain the character of its interior: the collection of box beds *in situ*; the use of furniture to divide people from animals; the insulation of a century of newspaper and wallpaper; and the 'hingin' lum' with a photograph of a previous occupant in the 1930s. Everyday artefacts – from working clothes to whisky bottles – are used to give visitors an idea of the character of the place. Since the atmosphere of the building has not been lost, and can still be appreciated by visitors, the Trust's conservation philosophy of minimal intervention appears to be successful.

The historic building survey and analysis of the 1702 laird's house at Old Auchentroig, Buchlyvie, provided an insight into the approach to its construction.[10] This attractive and architecturally significant building, whose imposing door was reputedly burnt during Rob Roy MacGregor's raid in 1710, was restored through the Trust's Little Houses Improvement Scheme and has been returned to domestic use. Old Auchentroig was believed to be an example of a rectangular laird's house, until examination of the roof structure and the rear wall revealed it to have had a rear extension. Having recorded the plans and elevations of the building, buildings archaeologist Tom Addyman studied the juxtaposition of the openings and fireplaces. He concluded that the structure was based on a grid of 3ft 9in – which later study showed to have been a standard measure in parts of Britain at the end of the seventeenth century.[11] Irregularities of symmetry can be accounted for by the internal positioning of furniture, such as the dresser.[12]

Restoration work at Holmwood House demanded detailed research and some archaeology outside the house, where the 1920s rose garden was known to have replaced something older. An archaeological evaluation followed, in which full-scale recording of the later features[13] preceded the stripping back of the garden to the original plan. It might seem strange to restore a simple vegetable garden within the curtilage of this architectural work of art, but this is what the architect intended, and it was not for us – in this case at least – to impose twentieth-century values on a nineteenth-century masterpiece.

One of the Trust's perhaps most unexpected domestic locations can be found underneath Culzean Castle where there is an extensive series of caves that were occupied for a time in the seventeenth century by Sir Archibald Kennedy of Culzean. The facade, which might at first sight seem to be a Robert Adam folly, turns out to be a piece of genuine medieval domestic architecture complete with garderobe. Sir Archibald was almost certainly not the first inhabitant of these fascinating caves, but the presence of giant cave-dwelling spiders dissuaded

Culzean Caves, home to Sir Archibald Kennedy of Culzean in the 17th century.
(NTS)

The Development of Scotland's Domestic Buildings

investigations by the Glasgow University Speleological Society during the 1960s. A less arachnophobic team is to return to investigate, also seeking the secret passage between the caves and the castle. It is sobering that Adam felt the need to prop up the castle above with two substantial stone columns.

Thus can scientific studies – including pollen analysis, radiocarbon dating and dendrochronology; scrutiny of maps, documents and oral testimony; traditional and novel uses of stratigraphic analysis; finds study and analysis; and historic buildings analysis – all assist in understanding the past. They are not solely archaeological techniques but reflect the association with many other disciplines, all of which come together in a combination that English Heritage puts under the generalised term 'buildings analysis'.[14] It has been a learning process, and will continue to be, as new challenges arise and new approaches evolve. Time and time again, archaeologists have played a critical role as part of the team of detectives whose job it is to record, understand and evaluate historic buildings and their environments. Collectively, under the banner of 'buildings analysts', we have only just begun to learn how best to tease out the story of the Scottish home and the people who built and lived in it.

Cairness House, near Fraserburgh, by James Playfair.

In the following section, Charles McKean suggests that a high proportion of Scottish homes are the result of adaptations of earlier structures, and that understanding the growth pattern of the house is central to understanding both the fabric and the changing lifestyles within.

Understanding the Scottish Home

Professor Charles McKean

Very few Scottish houses have not been altered or extended during their lifetimes. It is a natural condition, being the consequence of changing social habits, changing technology and changing social position – never mind the perennial desire to keep up with fashion. An architect newly returned from Rome with the latest trend? Everybody had to have a slice of him, or of his brother – failing whom, the spice of his assistant or indeed his office junior.[1] An architect returning from Revolutionary France (James Playfair) or, indeed, St Petersburg (William Stark), became instantly fashionable. Yet these fashionable architects were not always given a clear site. There was a predisposition in Scotland to continue on the same site and to adapt or rebuild what was already on it. Even now, negative equity tempts people to alter or extend rather than move. But the three architectural virtues of commodity, firmness and delight remain crucial in evaluating and understanding even alterations and adaptations to determine how the house developed as it appears today.

Caring for the Scottish home must begin with understanding the Scottish home (in the context of the overwhelming of the pre-1700 Scottish/European culture) by that of North Britain. Scotland's perennial fascination with utilising every new technology possible had the consequence, by the mid twentieth century, of erasing both knowledge and memory of our preceding technologies. So, if we had misunderstood our culture (our delight) and forgot our historic technologies (firmness), it cannot be altogether surprising that we should misunderstand how we used to live (commodity).

Since the predominant pre nineteenth-century technology in Scotland was load-bearing masonry, each alteration left its mark upon the building. Yet there still appears to be no systematic procedure for the analysis and understanding of architectural archaeology. Archaeological studies of buildings can, as a result, miss or misinterpret important features.[2] Moreover, we can have but an indifferent understanding of our country's historic culture if an *escalier d'honneur* can be dismissed as a 'turnpike', no matter how grand or ceremonial it is, just because it is circular;[3] or if it is forgotten that pre eighteenth-century buildings rarely have below-ground basements.[4] The requirement is to consider buildings or components of buildings in a logical manner, in the light of how they were used, and against the norms of that type of building or constructional feature. Newark Castle, Ayr, for example, is a tower, extended and then engulfed by later building. A proper understanding of the original tower must begin by asking questions such as 'where was (or is) the stair?' Two kitchens were discovered on the ground floor once work began to restore the Abbot's House in Dunfermline. It was initially suggested that hot food would be taken along corridors, out into the street, and up an external stair into the great chamber above. By the time of its arrival it would have been cold food. Rather, a massive piece of masonry approximately 10ft square in the corner of the kitchen seemed a likely candidate for the location of a now walled-up stair.

Balnain House, soon to be home to the Trust's Highland office.
(NTS)

Those designing and constructing our buildings even 600 years ago were highly skilled, and provided what their clients desired. They laid out their buildings to some discipline (probably geometric) and used the most efficient technology then locally available. Each building programme would have constant wall thicknesses appropriate to function; and as technology improved, wall thicknesses diminished. The biggest change occurred at the beginning of the sixteenth century when the planning of great houses changed from being vertical to horizontal. Stairs and subsidiary rooms, previously constrained within the thick walls, were expressed in structures coruscating from the exterior. Generally, wall thicknesses fell from 6ft plus to 4ft minus, and further to largely 3ft to 3ft 6in by the seventeenth century. One day it might even be possible to date buildings by wall thickness, although variables like the height of the building, walls containing chimney stacks, the number of storeys and the type of stone that was used will have to be factored in. William Adam, however, used a wall thickness of 2ft 10in for his subsidiary buildings;[5] Robert Adam seems to have preferred a wall thickness of 2ft 4in;[6] and William Burn 2ft 6in for walls with chimney flues, and 2ft otherwise.[7] An 1835 drawing of a proposed country house in Angus held in Dundee University Archives has walls with chimney flues of 3ft, and 2ft 4in otherwise.[8] So there never was universal consistency. Moreover, some architects tended to regularise wall thicknesses on their drawings, even where they varied in reality. When James Shearer was restoring the house of Brucefield between 1915 and 1922, his initial sketch survey showed substantial variations in wall thicknesses which implied that the house began with a small tower, was extended with a palace block in the sixteenth century, reformatted in the late seventeenth century, and completed to its current state in about 1724. Shearer's worked-up plans, however, regularised all the walls to the same thickness, concealing that history and implying it was all built at the same time: about 1724-8.[9] What can be relied on, however, is the probability that different wall thicknesses indicated the birth order of the house. Further clues to a house's building history will emerge from its plans and sections, in addition to what might be discovered on site.

Where the building is ruinous, changes in the type and bonding of stone are likely to be very much more significant to its construction history than, say, residual surviving plaster.[10] Evidence of past or present cracks or settlement can be crucial not just to understanding history, but also to potential problems. With so many alterations, slappings through, additions or removals, the structure of many buildings has been sorely tested, and such a crack might be a legacy – if not also a forecast of future problems. The east gable of the great tower at Pitsligo had been so perforated by two staircases and its great window that it fell out sometime in the eighteenth century.[11] The plans and sections of Balnain House in Inverness, for example, now impossible to inspect beneath its harl, imply that it is much older than its currently assumed eighteenth-century date. The thickness of some of its walls (3ft 6in to 4ft) is unusual for that period, and a central stairwell flanked by two enormously thick walls was much more common in the mid seventeenth century.[12] There are hints that the ground floor – now the restaurant floor – might originally have been vaulted. What was done in the eighteenth century was to re-cast the house as a beautiful unity, probably cannibalising what was there already.

Urban buildings can be even more complicated. There are remarkably few clues to the history of Gardyne's Lodging in Dundee's High Street, now gloriously transferred to the Tayside Building Preservation Trust, save the probability that there was once an arcaded timber projection to the High Street, removed along with the others in the mid eighteenth century.[13] Most of the internal clues were lost as a consequence of having been refitted out as offices in the 1960s. Archaeology revealed a thirteenth-century well and some very interesting finds in both Gray's Close and its unusual central courtyard. The building's plan, however, indicates the possibility of a very curious building history. The thickest walls encircle the open court at the centre and there is a rare post-and-beam timber structure of which one post is visible. In the evidentially seventeenth-century wall facing the close, the structure is extraordinarily thin. Moreover, the roof facing the High Street had been scarfed out, making it flatter, when a lovely panelled and plastered room with a buffet was installed about 1710. It seems probable that the complex comprised of tenements and booths facing the High Street and the typical courtyard merchant's house to the rear, opening from the close. An external stair would have lead to the first floor, with a corbelled turnpike stair taking you up to the floors above.[14] The inner walled courtyard is much less usual. There are no south-facing windows opening into the courtyard from the north range, and there is a large blocked-up opening leading from the court itself into the south range facing the High Street. The current working hypothesis, therefore, is that the courtyard represents the four walls of a hollowed-out stone tower, which may well have been the earliest building on this site.

In developing a methodology for considering standing architecture, we have not yet reached the standards achieved in the Netherlands,[15] with their analysis of timber-cutting techniques and dating. Nonetheless, the following, based on a practical test undertaken on Innes House, Morayshire, by a team of historic building specialists in April 1988, is suggested as a start.[16]

The first step is the *Study of Documentation* – relevant primary and secondary sources, manuscripts, local histories and family/genealogical histories; and whatever visual documentation – sketches, paintings, old town plans, drawings, architectural or feuing plans, or even the very large-scale 1850s Ordnance Survey –

Gardyne's Land, Dundee, *circa* 1895.

might be discovered. Victorian architectural plans, in particular, often highlight new work or alterations in a different colour. This material should provide a *Working Hypothesis* about the building. A *Detailed Inspection* follows, plotting all items that indicate a variation from the working hypothesis, into the *Schedule of Curiosities*. Then follows the *Analysis of the Schedule* – an attempt to unravel the logic behind each curiosity by testing them against both the relevant typology and whatever may exist in the documentation study. (For example, why should an apparently nineteenth-century cottage in Barnhill have a 4ft-thick wall? It transpired that the house in question had at least three different building periods, and probably more; one at least predating the nineteenth century.) Then follows the *Revisit* – a systematic inspection, floor by floor, function by function, curiosity by curiosity, best done in the opposite direction to the first inspection. Finally, a *Working Analysis* with tentative and broad conclusions will emerge, and the procedure ends with an identification of any further work that has been discovered.

It is best if the study involves those who know about masonry, plaster, harling, slate, iron, architectural history, social history and the sources of documentation. It is fundamentally a questioning, iterative process in which even the conclusions are likely to be provisional. The guiding spirit is to ask the question *why*? Why is it like this?

What is the relevance of this methodology for the future? An analysis of this kind should prove revealing about the nature of the building and its architectural significance, and prevent alterations to the building based on mythology. The revelations can sometimes be surprising. The next time you are watching the video at Kellie Castle in Fife, for example, you might be glad to know that there appear to be several feet of unsupported masonry cantilevered out over your head.

So what was the result of the Innes House study? The history of Innes is normally presented as a house new-built to a plan by William Ayton in 1644. It was chosen for study because the maps of Timothy Pont, possibly prepared in the 1590s,[17] showed a large (if somewhat old-fashioned) tower there. Had he depicted a different building on a different if nearby site, or did the tower still lurk within the current house? After a two-day analysis it was concluded that Ayton had provided a drawing of how to reformat and reorganise a substantial existing complex of tower, extension and sixteenth-century palace block by adding a new stairtower, reorganising floor levels and circulation, and creating a common roof level and new skyline. Innes House was later subjected to further significant alteration.

Where the building's architect has been identified, a study of their career, design motifs and approach to planning would be as significant as the study of the building itself. The current reconstructions of Queensberry House, for example, are based upon an approximate version of what Thomas Sandby drew in 1749. The house was, by then, over 50 years old, and long abandoned by the man who, when he built it, was the virtual ruler of Scotland. Moreover, these hesitant proposals do not begin to address how James Smith, that highly fashionable, Italian-trained architect with a fondness for a symmetrical composition rising to a noble apex at the centre, might actually have designed it to have looked from Arthur's Seat. It is insufficiently noble, and woefully so.

The mythology of many Scottish houses like the houses of Dun, Fasque, Foulis, Cromartie and others, is that these structures were new-built in the eighteenth century on new sites; and that some residual lump of masonry some distance away represents the sole relic and site of the predecessor. Occasionally, it is so; generally not. Scots clients preferred to re-use the thick walls of their existing

Gardyne's Land, Dundee, now in the care of Tayside Building Preservation Trust.

house. More often than not, old houses remain concealed in ghostly form beneath later fashioned facades.

Timothy Pont's 1596 map of Clydesdale indicates that many of what we now think of as inoffensive farmhouses of little pretension were, when drawn by him in the late sixteenth century, places of considerable significance. Such houses would not be bad places to begin testing this methodology.

References

The Development of Scottish Domestic Architecture in Cities, Towns and Villages

1   Thomas Girtin, *View of Jedburgh* (National Galleries of Scotland).
2   Sir John Sinclair, *The Statistical Account of Scotland* (1792), volume 1, p 472.
3   The catalogue of the exhibition is Timothy Clifford, *Designs of Desire* (National Galleries of Scotland 1999).
4   See Ian Gow, *The Scottish Interior* (1992), pp 161-2; and Glendinning *et al*, *A History of Scottish Architecture* (1998), pp 341-4.
5   Theodore Fontane has a good description of the yellow and green houses of Linlithgow, like those of his native Bavaria, in *Across the Tweed, Notes on Travel in Scotland* (1858). Translation (J M Dent and Sons, London 1965).
6   See RIAS (Royal Incorporation of Architects in Scotland), *Central Glasgow Guide*.
7   Quoted in A C Lamb, *Dundee – Its Quaint and Historical Buildings* (Dundee 1892).
8   Burn's Feu Plan is dated 7 February 1823 (Moncrieff Papers).
9   Reid's drawings are in the collection of the Duke of Atholl, 1806, in the NMRS (National Monuments Record of Scotland).
10 John Ruskin, *Lectures on Architecture and Painting delivered at Edinburgh in November 1853* (1854), p 76. For instance, the Moray estate: 14 Glenfinlas Street completed 1859, 10 and 11 St Colme Street completed 1858 – Ann Mitchell, *No More Corncraiks* (1998), pp 155-7. Turning to Playfair: Hillside Crescent was designed 1823, completed 1884 – Gifford, MacWilliam and Walker, *Buildings of Scotland – Edinburgh*, p 447. See also Ann Mitchell, *The People of Calton Hill* and *Buildings of Scotland – Edinburgh*, p 446. Both record buildings in Royal Terrace finished in 1860, but I think Hillside Crescent makes the point sufficiently well.
11 Glendinning *et al*, *A History of Scottish Architecture*, p 175.
12 Charles McKean, *Edinburgh, Portrait of a City* (1991), p 2.

Buildings of the Scottish Countryside

1   Edinburgh, 1985.
2   Catalogued under 'Buildings of the Scottish Countryside' in the NMRS.
3   Available at the NMRS in handwritten manuscript.
4   School of Scottish Studies at Edinburgh University, Old College, South Bridge, Edinburgh.
5   RCAHMS, 1997.
6   *Mar Lodge: The Archaeology of a Cairngorm Estate* (RCAHMS 1996).
7   Drawings held in the Bryce Collection of the NMRS.
8   Symonds are an Orcadian form of heather rope which is used to support heather thatch. The rope has to be rewoven by hand regularly. Traditionally a job for the long evenings of an Orcadian winter.

1   John Atkinson, Glasgow University Archaeological Research Division, personal communication.

2   Norman Emery, *Excavations on Hirta 1986-90* (1996).

3   Mary Harman, 'The History of St Kilda' in Meg Buchanan (ed), *St Kilda: The Continuing Story of the Islands* (Edinburgh, HMSO 1995), pp 18-19.

4   National Trust for Scotland (NTS) Management Plan, unpublished.

5   Kirkdale Archaeology, *The Bothy, Canna* (1997), unpublished report for NTS.

6   J L Campbell, *Canna: The Story of a Hebridean island* (third edition 1994), illustration 1 (Edinburgh, Canongate Books).

7   Kirkdale Archaeology, *The Bothy, Canna* (1997), unpublished report for NTS.

8   Addyman and Kay, *King's Stables Cottage* (1999), unpublished report for NTS.

9   Mairi Stewart, Highland Perthshire Nature Woodland, personal communication.

10   Addyman and Kay, in preparation.

11   Tom Addyman, personal communication. The measure was an ell of 3ft 9in (as opposed to a Scots ell of 3ft 1in).

12   Tom Addyman, personal communication.

13   Centre for Field Archaeology (1998/9), unpublished report.

14   English Heritage, *Conservation Based Recording and Analysis of Historic Buildings* (1999), unpublished internal conservation document.

Understanding the Scottish Home

1   Robert Adam spent 1754-8 in Italy, and his brother James may have been largely responsible for the firm's many Glasgow projects. After their deaths in 1792 and 1794, their chief assistant John Paterson picked up some of their clients; and thereafter David Hamilton, who appears to have been involved in the office in some capacity.

2   The report commissioned by the National Trust for Scotland, for example, on Alloa Tower was exhaustive in spotting certain items, but missed a section of wall unusually built in ashlar, and evidence of a large settlement crack.

3   David Jones, 'The Hall and the Lobby' in A Carruthers (ed), *The Scottish Home* (Edinburgh, NMS Publishing 1996), p 106. The staircase in question was the great stair at the House of Kinnaird.

4   Typologically, the basement functions in a pre-nineteenth century Scots house – cellars, kitchens and the like – generally took place at ground level. Sub-ground basements were rare, and usually only where a fall in the ground or other special circumstance required. Typologically, cellars in Scottish country houses were rubble built and plastered, barrel-vaulted and without ledges. From its rectangularity and ashlar walls and ledge, the 'basement' or cellar identified in Alloa Tower seems more likely to have been a cistern.

5   J Simpson (ed), *Vitruvius Scoticus* (Edinburgh 1980), plan of Floors.

6   James Simpson, Ian Begg and Stewart Todd, 1993, personal correspondence.

7   William Burn drawings in NMRS, particularly those of Invergowrie House and Duntrune House.

8   Dundee University Archives: manuscript volume in the Cox collection of plans and elevations for a house in Angus, unsigned and probably an amateur hand.

9   Plans held by Lord Balfour of Burleigh in Brucefield.

10   See note 2 above.

11   Charles McKean, 'The House of Pitsligo' in *PSAS 121* (Edinburgh 1991).

12   As at Methven, for example, constructed *c.*1678, probably by James Smith.

13   *Dundee Delineated* (Dundee 1822).

14   A number of examples of this type of courtyard house are illustrated in A C Lamb, *Dundee, its quaint and historic buildings* (Dundee 1886).

15   Koos Streehouwer, *The construction history of historic buildings,* translated by S van Es and A C Cumming (Dundee 1998). Books like J Wood (ed), *Buildings Archaeology* do not address the analytical approach based upon typology suggested in this paper. A focus upon a stylistic approach to architectural history can be misleading.

16   They were James Simpson, Ian Gow, Ian Davidson, Ted Ruddock, Kitty Cruft, Peter Donaldson, Neil Grieve and Charles McKean, ably hosted and assisted by Hermione Tennant, with Joe and Carol Innes and Blair Brookes.

17   In the Map Library, National Library of Scotland.

To undertake the appropriate repair and maintenance needs of the Scottish home requires an effective combination of knowledge, skill and materials. Emphasise any one of these factors over the others, and less than satisfactory work will result. This chapter investigates the current and emerging issues associated with such a problem.

The opening section by Ingval Maxwell, Director of the Technical Conservation Research and Education Division, Historic Scotland, looks at the Scottish scene from a European perspective and identifies the scope and amount of repair and maintenance work required to bring the domestic housing stock into a good condition. It notes the attempts to return to the marketplace an understanding and supply of traditional materials, and the conflicts that can occur when new materials are unthinkingly brought on stream. It also considers the growing skill shortage and looks at what is being done by the Scottish Stone Liaison Group to address this issue.

Bruce Walker, Senior Lecturer, University of Dundee, brings forward a compelling case that many Scottish roofs were originally covered with timber shingles. Looking at and reinterpreting the evidence with fresh eyes, it is difficult not to be swayed by the emerging argument. His call to search for more evidence should not be lightly dismissed.

The case studies in masonry work presented by Bob Heath, of Heath Architect and Stone Consultant, raise a number of philosophical and ethical issues that the practitioner should consider in the repair of traditional stone-built structures. While acknowledging that no simple, straightforward answer will ever be applicable, he stresses the need to come to terms with the more ephemeral aspects of conservation work before the practical stages get underway.

If there is one area of traditional building work currently gaining considerable popularity, it must be the field of lime technology. Pat Gibbons, Director, Scottish Lime Centre Trust, offers a pragmatic insight into lime as a material. Developing the themes set out by Bob Heath, her argument for its greater use in building repair works is both logical and relevant.

Ben Tindall, Partner, Benjamin Tindall Architects, offers a broad-ranging introduction to the use and development of timber in the Scottish home. Taking each element in turn, he follows up by promoting a greater adoption of Society for the Protection of Ancient Buildings' repair philosophies and techniques.

As a protective (often sacrificial) coating, paints are frequently omitted from serious debates on the care of historic buildings. Peter Maitland Hood, Consultant Surveyor, Peter Maitland Hood/Hood Stilling, addresses this failure. Through his insight and knowledge of the topic, much evidence is offered on both a practical and academic level. Performance needs are understood, as are the clues that can aid the identification and dating of relevant colour schemes.

The chapter aggregates to a body of knowledge and information not easily found elsewhere.

The Old Schoolhouse, Cottown. A good example of thatch, clay walls and lime plastering.
(NTS)

Culross Palace, Fife.
(NTS)

Traditional Materials and Repair

Editor: Ingval Maxwell

Sourcing Traditional Materials and Skill Requirements for the Repair of Scotland's Domestic Architecture

Ingval Maxwell

Rosemarkie. Note the profiled gable raggle to accommodate thatch covering of the demolished house on the right, and the over-sailing eaves, barge board and sheet covering of the single-storey thatched cottages on the left.
(INGVAL MAXWELL)

Monaive. Regional differences are evident with deeper building plans, shallower roof pitches, a greater use of wall surface paint and larger diminishing course slater-work.
(INGVAL MAXWELL)

Scottish traditional domestic buildings provide a panoply of variations. With most pre-1900 buildings this appears in the range of colours, textures and forms which are in evidence where climatic, geological and functional factors were addressed and accommodated in the design and built detail.

From the point of view of repair and maintenance, this diversity creates a range of problems, especially where the need to replace an original piece of the construction emerges. While most traditional materials perform well, with anticipated life often far exceeding design life, some will fail through the demands that are placed on them. This failure might be aggravated by inappropriate previous work such as stone-cleaning, or be a result of a disaster such as fire. Whatever the reason, if sympathetic repairs are to be carried out, they are best exercised through the adoption and specification of materials that match the original as closely as possible. In the current climate, however, adopting such an approach does create dilemmas. While it may be a simple task to make demands of 'originality', it is becoming increasingly difficult to achieve them in practice.

A frequently quoted statistic that emphasises this difficulty concerns the availability of building stone. In the heyday of Scottish masonry construction 150 years ago, some 1200 quarries are estimated to have been producing building-quality stone. Currently there are only 20 in operation. Inevitably, the choice of material is much more limited than that originally available. This highlights two important issues. First, there is an inescapable requirement to ensure that the remaining traditional building stock is more fully appreciated and more carefully attended. Second, where replacement work is necessary, it needs very careful handling to ensure that the quality of the original is not reduced through the use of inappropriate components.

In addition, as modern building technology has moved to adopt a greater use of quality-controlled, factory-manufactured precision units, the loss of an effective craft skill base to deal with traditional construction has become all but critical. Fortunately, there is an increasing awareness of the need to understand this complex predicament.

From the broader perspective, the European Commission Co-operation in Science and Technology (COST) Action C5 *Urban Heritage – Building Maintenance* study has taken as its challenge the aim of quantifying the extent of repair needs of existing buildings throughout Europe. A programme involving eleven member states was initiated in 1996 and, after three years of concentrated work, the Action compiled its findings for a final presentation in October 2000. For the first time this offered an overview of the scale of the European problem.

Six different Working Groups operating under the control of a co-ordinating Management Committee were set up to carry out the plans of the Action. By bringing together such a broad range of interest and work activities, a comprehensive understanding of the pan-European issues has now started to emerge.

The aim of Working Group 1 on the 'Criteria and Current Methods of

Evaluation' was to ascertain the systems used to establish data in each country; to collect data concerning the quantity of urban heritage (on the number and size of buildings, *etc*); to collect data concerning the condition of buildings and renovation measures; and to discover which groups of buildings have to be repaired (to project the total demand for repairs and their urgency). The first step was to identify and assess the various national institutions concerned with building stock documentation. As a result it was found that while available data related predominantly to residential buildings, no country produced comprehensive documentation. Against this background the group concluded that the creation of an effective database of the building stock and its physical condition is an absolute necessity to aid the appropriate preservation and repair of the urban heritage.

Due to the complexity and scale of the issues likely to be encountered in the omnibus topic *Urban Heritage – Building Maintenance*, Working Group 1A on 'Framework Evaluation Criteria' devised a structured framework within which the intentions and remit of the Action could be accommodated, linked and developed.

Working Group 2 on 'Inspection and Diagnosis' embarked on the task of determining what condition the buildings were actually in. Due to the timescale for the Action, work concentrated on the technical aspects of re-strengthening foundations and addressing various building materials. A collection of case-study information was also part of the intentions and this was followed by the identification of non-destructive/destructive testing techniques.

Edinburgh. Most Scottish stone buildings are designed to throw water away from the underlying wall face. Best seen performing while it is raining, projecting eaves courses and string mouldings at different levels all act in unison in this function.
(INGVAL MAXWELL)

Operating in conjunction with Working Group 2, Working Group 3 ('Methods and Techniques of Rehabilitation') aimed to identify, delineate and study problem areas in which specific techniques of improvement could be applied. Jointly the groups arranged a state-of-the-art International Congress at Delft University of Technology in the Netherlands in October 1999. Proceedings were published on 'Foundations', 'Concrete' and 'Iron and Steel'. A further event was planned for Zurich in October 2000 when 'Stone', 'Plaster', 'Timber' and 'Brick' were investigated.

In November 1997 a new group, Working Group 4 on 'International Co-ordination', was given the task of developing co-ordination and awareness of other international issues that were of relevance to COST Action C5. The work was to take a number of directions, noting related activities in the following areas: general awareness; study tours and visits; specific reports and papers; research initiatives; current research activities; conferences and seminars.

Tollcross House, Glasgow. An 1848 Baronial house by David Bryce, sympathetically converted into flats in 1989 with due regard to both external and internal detail.
(INGVAL MAXWELL)

At the inaugural meeting in November 1997 it was considered that there was a need to establish a fuller European understanding of the use of lime in the maintenance and care of the urban built heritage. As a result, agreement was reached on the need to prepare a database of relevant information. The Scottish Lime Centre Trust agreed to co-ordinate the work on behalf of Working Group 5 on 'Lime Technology'. A questionnaire was drawn up and circulated to contacts across Europe and a wide range of responses obtained. By February 1998 over 200 replies had been received as a result of the initiative. Almost 110 of these had been submitted from the United Kingdom, revealing the clear benefits of a properly organised network (the United Kingdom's Buildings Lime Forum) as a vehicle for information gathering and dissemination. An overview of the current use of lime in Europe was also presented at an international workshop in Mainz, Germany, in May (with Eurolime), and in Stockholm, Sweden, in September 1998. It is hoped that publications will ultimately emerge as a result of these initiatives.

While we have detailed statistics on the European dimension regarding cars,

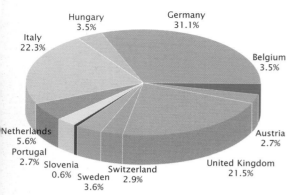

Fig 1: Distribution profile of the European Dwelling Stock by the eleven participating COST Action C5 countries (112,576,000 dwelling units in total). (Source: COST Action C5)

Downpipe and sandstone wall. With a porosity of 15-24% sandstone structures can absorb a considerable amount of water if it is concentrated onto it. If the situation is left to its own devices, this loading can readily transmit a great deal of moisture through the build from the external face to the interior. Traditional construction normally utilises the application of many timber wedges driven directly into the interior masonry wall-face joints, to which the finishing lath and plaster of the room is applied. Where water is allowed to reach this zone the risk of dry rot occurring is high. Simple replacement of the broken cast iron pipe section would have remedied the situation.

(INGVAL MAXWELL)

butter and wine, we actually know little about the real state of our buildings! However, as a result of the Action's work, it is currently estimated that the dwelling stock of Austria, Belgium, Germany, Hungary, Italy, the Netherlands, Portugal, Slovenia, Sweden, Switzerland and the United Kingdom is 112.5 million dwelling units (figures for France are excluded as they were not a member of the Action).

Arranged by date, 20.5% of all dwellings were built pre-1919, 15% in 1919-45, 30% in 1946-70, 28% in 1971-90, and the rest since 1991. In the United Kingdom it is estimated that 28.8% of homes were built pre-1919 (the highest of all the eleven countries in the COST Action C5 programme), followed by Austria at 22.5% and Germany at 20.4%. The use of traditional building materials in the United Kingdom will therefore feature as a significant issue in the repair and maintenance sector of the construction industry for some time to come.

Minimum maintenance, refurbishment and renovation costs have been more difficult to establish. However, emerging data from Flanders, Germany, Scotland and Northern Ireland indicates that a basic average repair cost per dwelling is approximately 2700 euros. Taking the estimated 112.5 million units in the survey area across Europe, a current repair bill is projected at over 303.5 billion euros. Given this projection, understanding and implementing sustainability is essential. If sufficient associated technical information were also readily available, such statistics would help create an appropriate base for pre-planning purposes to give indications of material supply requirements and skill demands.

On the Scottish scene, relevant information was made available by the published results of the 1996 *Scottish House Condition Survey*. A one per cent actual on-site survey by qualified surveyors, this analysis was undertaken as part of the 1996 quinquennial Scottish Homes Research Project. With a force of 250 interviewers and 130 surveyors and surveyor supervisors, over 20,000 households were involved in the largest-ever research project carried out in Scotland. From a wealth of data, the analysed information offers a considerable insight into the future repair needs of the housing stock.

The survey commenced in February 1996 and built upon the findings of the previous 1991 study. It occasioned an external and internal inspection survey of each property and a socio-economic interview with the householder. The physical survey focused on characteristics of the stock: the types of materials used in construction; whether the dwelling met the statutory tolerable standard; the presence of damp and condensation; the requirement for internal and external repairs; the residual life of building components; thermal efficiency; whether the dwelling conformed with barrier-free standards; what amenities were lacking; and the standard of services and fittings. The findings on state of disrepair and residual life expectations are of particular relevance. They are particularly important for future planning, given that they can be used to project future material supply needs and training demands.

By way of example, the analysis identified that 1,648,000 dwellings (78% of the total stock) had at least one item of visible disrepair, with over 250,000 houses requiring remedial work to their principle roof coverings, gutters, downpipes, external wall finishes, fireplaces, flues or external steps.

In projecting residual life expectancy it was estimated that within the next ten years replacement work will be required on 128,000 principal roof covers (6%); 207,000 secondary roof covers (42%); 370,000 external doors (18%); 394,000 external windows (19%); 304,000 flashings (14%); and 247,000 gutters (12%). In addition it was projected that 55% of the principal roof covers, 80% of secondary roof covers, 46% of chimney stacks, and 34% of external stairs will need to be replaced within 30 years.

If constructional details and methods of building are taken into account, it is a relatively simple exercise to extrapolate associated needs from these figures. It should be possible to project the future material supply and craft skill needs required to satisfy the pending demands of repair and maintenance programmes. With such an insight it should also be possible for suppliers and training providers to start planning activities that will be required to meet the anticipated demand. Unfortunately the building industry, material suppliers, education providers and training establishments have generally not been aware of the value of this work. As a result the study findings remain greatly underused – more needs to be done to promote them.

The emerging European and detailed Scottish perspectives provide corroboration of related Department of the Environment, Transport and the Region (DETR) information. This shows that a national 50/50 split between repair and maintenance/new build in the construction industry annual spend has been in existence for some time. The clear implication is that maintenance will remain a high priority in the construction industry for the foreseeable future. In fact, some hold that the repair and maintenance sector is on the increase. Should this prove to be the case, a greater awareness of the consequences is required and a number of associated aspects have to be more fully appreciated. Assuming that the original design integrity of our buildings has some relevance for the future, failure to consider this will inevitably have an adverse effect on the quality and appearance of the stock. Although it is accepted that the core argument may be more relevant to 'historic' structures, a traditionally built house of similar age does not need to be 'listed' to have the same design qualities, constructional details, materials, maintenance problems or needs as its 'listed' counterpart.

The need to undertake effective repair and maintenance work requires a number of issues to come together if the quality of the building is not to suffer. These must remain in balance throughout the process. Associated case study findings can greatly assist practitioners in the operation as they can help to quantify material supply needs, prepare training requirements, determine back-up educational needs and accommodate regional variations. Unfortunately there is a considerable misapprehension in the industry regarding the appropriate use of traditional building materials. This makes it necessary to produce and publish a range of technical support documents, some of which should be in the form of case studies.

In recent years a range of relevant Scottish technical publications has appeared, following the style and approach of the trend-setting Edinburgh New Town Conservation Committee (ENTCC) *The Care and Conservation of Georgian Houses: A Maintenance Manual*, first published in 1975. In particular, the series of 15 sections of the Glasgow West Conservation Trust *Conservation Manual*, released over the last eight years, do for Victorian domestic buildings what the ENTCC did for Georgian dwellings.

Historic Scotland's Technical Conservation Research and Education Division (TCRE) entered the field in 1992 and has produced a series of Technical Advice Notes, Practitioners' Guides, Conference Proceedings and Research Reports. These aim to address the current high levels of loss – loss of understanding, awareness, knowledge and skills. Topics addressed so far include developing a historic perspective of material supplies; understanding the technology of traditional materials; and understanding craft working techniques.

If water leaks in traditional buildings are left unattended the consequences are inevitable. Much structural damage can occur before outbreaks of dry rot are dealt with. The fungus can rapidly spread in the ideal conditions that exist for it in the relatively dead air-spaces behind lath and plaster work and timber panelling.
(INGVAL MAXWELL)

Perth, window-cill bush. It is remarkable how often obvious defects can be allowed to develop without any form of remedial action being undertaken. Uncleared established growth and debris in gutters that prevents the effective discharge of collected rainwater is common-place. Other problems centre on how well growth can establish itself in the most unusual places. A stitch-in-time housekeeping maintenance approach is always beneficial in such circumstances.
(INGVAL MAXWELL)

The publications also concentrate on the materials and their designed use in individual types of building. Particularly, *The Conservation and Conversion of Rural Buildings in the Lothians: Practitioners Guide*, the *Hebridean Blackhouse* and the pending *Old Schoolhouse, Cottown* offer detailed analysis of practical projects. As such, they aim to advance current thinking in the area and provide a platform upon which more detailed study and investigation can develop.

During the Historic Scotland 'Traditional Buildings Materials' conference in 1997 it was proposed that in the pre-industrial era the distance range from which such materials were collected amounted to not much more than 400 yards from the actual site of the building.

With regard to the more vernacular usage of materials, research generally supports that contention. However, developments in the canal and railway network greatly influenced and expanded material availability and use. International trade is a factor that always influenced Scottish buildings, but as the Industrial Revolution progressed this too expanded enormously. It was a two-way process: Scottish stone to Europe and America, with Baltic timbers and Vermont slates in return. More research needs to be carried out into the range of exchanges and the mechanisms by which they were initiated and deployed. In the meantime, a greater range of materials is now being imported and appears to be on the increase. Unfortunately they do not always offer the specifier and end user an appropriate choice from which effective maintenance and repairs can be achieved.

This calls for a detailed understanding of all materials in use, their performance, decay processes and, perhaps more importantly, where to find renewal sources to undertake matching repairs – if at all possible. With many original material sources no longer available as a result of landfill, urban development and lack of investment, or simply through being worked out, a major problem is currently facing the industry sector, compounded by the diminution of the traditional skill base. No single organisation can address all the issues. So, if progress is to be made, a concerted approach of all interested partners is called for.

As the need to undertake more maintenance work develops, so too does the need to appreciate what factors contributed to the building as a whole. Few alternatives exist. Lack of original sourcing leads to compromise and a reduction in the integrity of the structures as alternative and synthetic materials are used in the repair process. Interestingly, many of the modern-day synthetic replacements refer to the past for an identity and an implied quality status. The search for this marketable identity can be readily seen in the text of adverts in the current technical journals. Many fall back on projecting the proven quality of materials of the past to give the modern products enhanced credibility. To fully address the quality of our built heritage stock, the factor of authenticity must be considered to a greater degree. While modern synthetic replacement materials might be attractive on considerations of economies of scale and initial value for money, the question must be whether that initial assessment still holds good if life-cycle costing is taken into account. Some examples reveal the problem.

In the flourishing world of the replacement window industry, how often is thought given to the fact that windows that may have had a life of over 150 years are discarded to be replaced by units that are pushed to provide a 30-year guarantee? How often do salesmen explain that the buildings' original windows could last another 150 years if properly repaired, but the replacement units will have to be replaced a further four times over that expected lifespan?

West Lothian farm cottages. Even the most basic of conversions can dramatically alter the appearance of a building. The loss of a chimney, inappropriate window proportions, unsympathetic fenestration designs, and blocked-up masonry all contribute to an overall loss of character and detail.
(INGVAL MAXWELL)

Cottown clay pit. Recognition of the value of clay as a building material, and an awareness of its quality and suitability for use, was generally behind the decision to build near the supply. The partially water-filled depression reveals the location of the clay-pit source. Through the use of manual labour the commodity was economically exploited to maximum effect in the construction of the adjacent property.
(INGVAL MAXWELL)

Similarly, in hard landscaping projects, what is the actual life expectancy of synthetic brick paviours laid as a direct replacement of discarded original granite or whin paving setts? In this case the equation might give the manufactured unit only 25 years of performance against a timeless value for the natural materials that were discarded. Finally, through a lack of understanding as to how sandstone buildings perform in the elements, many structures now suffer from the consequences of being brush-coated with a 'magic formula' waterproofer or consolidant. By trying to emulate in minutes what nature took many millions of years to achieve, such an ill-informed approach often exacerbates any underlying problems. Subsequent repair needs are also greatly, and unnecessarily, complicated.

With 'sustainability' issues and 'energy efficiency' arguments emerging from the shadows, the question of real 'life-cycle costing' deliberations must start featuring to a greater degree in the consideration of clients and specifiers. Add to this the scale of the skill issue that needs to be addressed, and the real level of concern starts to emerge.

Recent Construction Industry Training Board (CITB) data on available skills for 2000-4 forecasts a Scottish shortage in bricklaying, plastering, scaffolding, roof-slating and tiling trades. This projection is set against 1998 statistics for the UK where only 3765 stonemasons were recorded against 117,715 bricklayers and 1488 in facade cleaning and maintenance. Given the high proportion of pre-1919 buildings built of stone and in need of appropriate maintenance, these statistics alone give great cause for concern. They demonstrate that the skills deployed in the repair and maintenance sector of the construction industry can be badly mismatched. Such a deficiency can only result in a diminution of the attributes of the building, as appropriately trained craftsmen may not be available to undertake quality repair work. Considering trainee numbers in what might be thought of as traditional skills, the detailed pattern in the current CITB study does not appear to ease this situation.

Dalbeattie windows and dormers. In a townscape, the aggregated effect of a variety of lost original details from a number of individual properties can have a profoundly negative effect on the whole.
(INGVAL MAXWELL)

Trade situation for 1998–99	All UK intake	Scottish intake 1999-2000	Scottish needs 2000-2004
Carpentry and Joinery (incl Bench Joinery)	12805	820	1300
Bricklaying	6683	227	550
Painting and Decorating	4461	276	370
Plumbers	4316	N/A	560
Plastering (incl Fibrous Plastering)	1279	47	150
Roof Slating and Tiling	267	(incl Sheet) 104	180
Scaffolding	209	72	70
Stonemasonry	172	21	–
Glazing	54	18	30
Steeplejacks	0	N/A	–

Fig 2: Enrolment in UK construction courses in 1998-99, set against the Scottish intake for 1999-2000 and the projected average annual requirement for 2000-04 [CITB source + Scottish intake figures for 1999-2000 sourced by the Scottish Stone Liaison Group, December 1999]

Traditional Materials and Repair

Due to the geographical distribution of facilities there are large areas of Scotland where no college-based skills provision exists. The Northern and Western Isles, South-West and Borders are particularly affected. In some areas potential trainees are required to travel considerable distances to secure the necessary underpinning knowledge. It is recognised that for some less-than-mainstream skills this will always be the position, but it is equally acknowledged that primary core skills should be available locally. Often this is not the case and fundamental trades such as plastering, roofing, glazing and scaffolding fall into this category. Lack of training also risks a bleeding of expertise into the city markets. Such a displacement could potentially aggravate the present deficit and impact further on the lack of skills availability.

From the point of view of the integrity of buildings constructed with stone, the abysmal state of the masonry trade in particular is dire. There is too much at stake for its plight to be ignored for much longer. A further problem exists. Currently college management advises that they require a minimum class size of twelve trainees to ensure the viability of a course. Assuming a 10% dropout rate over the year, the actual minimum intake level needs to stand at 14 or higher. Within the 1999-2000 Scottish intake total of 1793 students, 58% of college courses on offer started the year with 14 or fewer students. A greater awareness of the consequences of this situation must register in the minds of clients and others involved in planning for the future of the industry.

Fortunately, the masonry-related problem has been recognised and a number of bodies are working together to address the issues. With a pan-industry membership, one of the most active is the Scottish Stone Liaison Group (SSLG) which, with clearly defined aims and objectives, is systematically approaching the range of issues that need to be resolved. Working in pan-topic areas of mutual interest, positive developments are emerging on the basis of a shared understanding of the topics and associated problems.

Historic Scotland's major conference on *Traditional Building Materials* in September 1997 promoted a significant number of related projects. These spanned the entire range of traditional materials: timber, lime, earth, clay, brick, thatch and stone. A research report by Hutton & Rostron, entitled *A Future for Stone in Scotland*, was also presented. This study was steered through to gestation by the multi-disciplinary, integrated work of the SSLG. The report findings underlined the current problems encountered by the industry and highlighted a variety of issues that the built heritage faces.

In particular, the loss of a large number of building stone quarries was acknowledged to be a serious sourcing problem, as material from the remaining outlets is often inappropriate to match other sources. Many major original quarries have become worked out, infilled, built over, urban locked, or are currently used as landfill sites. In many cases it is virtually impossible for them to re-open. However in recent years, for some very specific projects, it has proved possible with particular environmental conditions to adopt 'snatch quarrying' techniques on closed, but still accessible, quarry faces. As a result of this approach, appropriate repair work has been carried out at Châtelherault, Hamilton; the Custom House, Dundee; and on the Scott Monument, Edinburgh.

It is also necessary to ensure the economic viability of current commercial quarrying operations to continue to provide matching indigenous material where appropriate. Failure to do so will see replacements being increasingly sourced from countries as diverse as Brazil, India and China. If this process continues, it is inevitable that repairs to the existing building stock will be compromised.

The immediate work of the SSLG aims to continue to pull together all aspects of the Scottish stone industry so that it becomes a more effective, cohesive and meaningful force. To help achieve this, an industry-wide integrated business plan has been developed, designed to promote confidence in meeting the different challenges. Founded on the Hutton & Rostron Report, the plan proposes a management committee to oversee the activities of three project teams. Each team would address a specific part of the plan, develop its intentions, and report progress to the management committee from which it can take further guidance. In addition, the creation of a Scottish-based 'Natural Stone Institute' is seen as essential to success. Through trying to ensure the availability of materials for future work, the committee will focus on enhancing the skills and education of both operatives and professionals. By building upon the range of available indigenous materials and developing professional and craft skills, enhanced by the introduction of modern working practices, industry expansion is a real possibility.

Currently organisations and professional bodies are being brought up to date and made aware of the changes in the structure and aims of the SSLG, which will help to ensure that the proposals of the Hutton & Rostron Report can be realised as fully as possible. Much needs to be done, but with the continuing commitment, assistance and support provided by the various bodies in SSLG membership, much more will be possible. The shared 'vision' is the creation of an environment that supports a healthy and sustainable Scottish stone industry in the future.

To undertake appropriate repair and maintenance work, a number of issues must be effectively integrated if the quality of a building is not to suffer. Unfortunately there is considerable misunderstanding regarding the effective use of traditional building materials. The recognition of training and educational needs must run hand-in-hand with material supply requirements. With many original material sources no longer available, a major supply problem currently faces the industry sector. No single organisation can address all these issues, but through working together to promote the current range of available traditional materials and the development of linked skills, a meaningful resolution of the difficulties in this area of work is emerging as a real prospect.

Locharbriggs Quarry, Dumfries. Although the overall number of operating building stone quarries in Scotland has reduced, those that remain have exploited modern technology to good effect. Such advances offer comforting assurance that some of the required materials will continue to be available in the future. (INGVAL MAXWELL)

The Use of Shingles on Scottish Roofs

Bruce Walker

The predominant roofing material in Scotland from the prehistoric period to about 1900 was thatch. This does not mean that there was a single material covering all roofs in the country. They were covered with a range of vegetable materials including seaweeds, straight-stemmed plants such as bracken, dock, irises, reeds, rushes, natural grasses and cultivated cereals; and woody plants such as broom, juniper and heather. This list is not exhaustive – the final choice of material was dependent on site location, degree of exposure, roof pitch, local farming practise, local economy, the number of helpers available, and many other factors. The choice

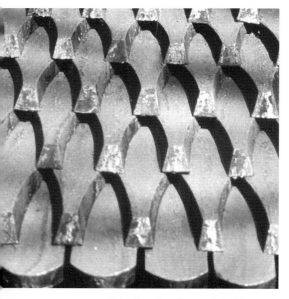

Fishtail and scallop ended shingles, Fortun (Fantoft, Bergen) stave-church, Norway.
(BRUCE WALKER)

Scallop and point ended shingles with ridge cresting and dragon-head finish, Borgund stave-church, Norway.
(BRUCE WALKER)

is not always easy to understand in relation to present-day criteria, but the range of thatching materials, methods of application, anchoring devices, and so on, was limitless. Gradually, as construction firms began to replace volunteer labour, the range of thatches reduced, but even then an extremely wide choice was available. Thatch types surviving into the twentieth century have been studied[1] and guidance has been provided for their repair and renewal. Many Scottish thatches required periodic resurfacing to ensure their continued performance. This results in a stratified accumulation, and by using archaeological techniques on the roof covering we have been able to identify changes in the husbandry of thatching materials over successive decades.[2]

Thatch was so common that 'tack' or 'thatch' became a generic term for any roofing material. Other materials were used from Roman times onwards, but only for very high-status buildings. Even as late as the eighteenth century, reference is often made to a building being 'thatched with' slate, stone, tile, timber or some other material. In high-status building reports these new materials were often referred to as 'scailie', 'scailyie', 'scailze' or 'skailie'. The spelling is fairly close to 'sclait', 'sclate' or slate, and this has caused further confusion; but Imrie and Dunbar say that 'scailie' refers equally to a covering of slate, stone, tile or timber that is blue slate, grey slate, plain-tile or shingle.[3]

Although all these materials were known and used during the Roman occupation of Britain, there is no evidence of any large-scale activity in the production of blue slate, grey slate, or roof tile in Scotland until the mid eighteenth century. This leaves shingles as the only roofing material that could be produced in any quantity without leaving physical evidence on the environment. Other materials gradually being introduced, such as lead, copper, paper and iron, were costly to produce and most were not available in sheet form until the later medieval or post-medieval periods. Shingle appears to be the material that naturally bridges the gap between the early thatches and the roofing materials currently covering large-scale high-status buildings such as cathedrals, churches, castles, palaces and government buildings.

The medieval sources of scailie for royal buildings, such as Edinburgh Castle, Stirling Castle, Holyrood House and Linlithgow Palace, are given as Aberfoyle and Dunkeld. Both areas were known for slate production in the nineteenth century, but were heavily wooded in the medieval period. The lack of evidence for early quarries and the difficulties encountered in extracting Scottish slate suggest that timber shingles were being used. This is supported by documentary evidence from England, where it is known that churches as large as Salisbury Cathedral were shingled when first erected and the shingles were only replaced after lead sheets of sufficient size for roofing purposes became readily available.[4]

Turning away from the documentary evidence to consider some of the early stone monuments found in Scotland, we see that many of the Class 2 Pictish stones depict crosses made from brushwood – they are copies of basketwork structures. This was recently confirmed by the late Alistair Smart, sculptor, while producing a replica of the Pictish cross-slab from Fowlis Wester, Perthshire. He demonstrated that although there was an underlying geometry to the pattern on the stone, each strand was off-set to allow for the thickness of the osiers and it is impossible to set out the pattern mechanically. This, combined with the accuracy of some of the incised carving on both Class 1 and Class 2 stones, suggested a high degree of observation in carving from nature or from an existing object. Assuming a similar level of artistic expertise for other stone monuments from the same period, the hog-backed tombstones stand out as reasonable depictions of contemporary buildings. They show a range of walled buildings with hog-backed roofs with bestial finials at one or both ends of the ridge. The carving of the wattled panels forming the walls is accurate but out of scale with the entire structure, and the same can be said of the roof covering. The roof carving appears to depict timber shingles of the Nordic type, as can still be seen on the stave-churches of Norway and many later buildings in Sweden and other Baltic countries. The hog-backed roof form is the same general type as survives on Historic Scotland's Blackhouse at 42 Arnol, Lewis, but with the roof covered with shingles. Different stones depict different types of shingle, but each type corresponds exactly with a type still surviving in Scandinavia.

Sceptics may consider the apparent link between the hog-backed tombstones and Norwegian stave-churches to be tenuous. However, many of the excavated Viking longhouses at sites such as Jarlshof in Shetland would, from their plan form, have had hog-backed roofs, and the oldest surviving stave-church in the world is at East Grinstead, Essex.[5] The shingle types known in Scandinavia can be classified as: lancet, scalloped, pointed, straight-tailed and fish-tailed. These are pine shingles and are thick at the butt edge although quite narrow in proportion to their length. The author regrets not having measured replacement shingles being put on a medieval church at Sigtuna, Sweden in 1984.

Pine shingles from the Nordic countries are quite different in character to the oak shingles of Central Europe and it is the oak-shingle technique that is found in England. There the documentary evidence for shingles goes back to the twelfth century, when Alexander Neckham stated that a hall might be roofed with straw, rushes, shingles or tiles ('chaume, ros, cengles, teules'). Wooden tiles were used at Dover Castle in 1220-1;[6] Kennington and Woodstock were shingled in 1248;[7] and Westminster Abbey in 1259.[8] In 1260 Henry III ordered that the thatch be removed from the outer chamber of the high tower of Marlborough Castle and replaced with shingles;[9] Clarendon 'aula domini regis indiget coopertura scindulavum' in 1272;[10] and shingles were used at Walmer, Hants in 1285.[11]

There are other examples from the early Middle Ages: Salisbury Cathedral was roofed with shingles from the Bramshaw Woods in the New Forest; and twelve oak trees from Sherwood Forest were sent to the Franciscans in Lincoln for shingles.[12] At Lincoln the shingles were copied on the weathering copes of the buttresses in the thirteenth century. This practice of copying the texture of the roof on the buttress copes was more common on the Continent than in England.[13] The author has noted this practice at Roslin Chapel, Midlothian, but has not been able to establish a date for that part of the building. C F Innocent appears to believe that the use of shingles did not last beyond the end of the fourteenth century: 'In the year 1314 it was found that certain of the royal manor houses and castles which were roofed with wooden shingles might be roofed at a less cost with stone slates or earthen tiles.'[14]

In 1688, R Holme defined shingling as a mode of roofing with cleft wood, about 6 to 8in broad and 12in long (150-200mm x 300mm). These are slightly wider but considerably shorter than the Scandinavian pine shingles and are 'pinned at one end to hang on the laths. They are laid as slates with moss under them, which is termed mouseing'.[15]

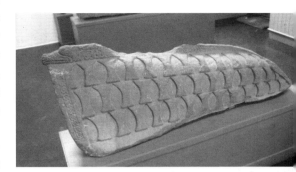

Hog-backed tombstone with curved representations of fishtail ended shingles, cresting and dragon head, Meigle, Perthshire.
(BRUCE WALKER)

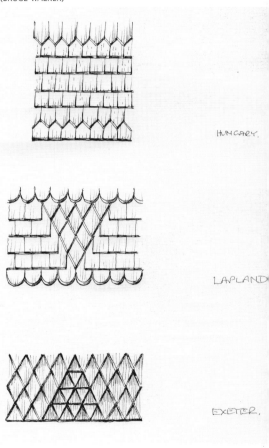

Examples of decorative shingle patterns from Hungary, Lapland and Exeter.
(BRUCE WALKER)

In England the use of shingles is now confined to church spires, particularly in the south-east of the country. This proves that the technique was not totally abandoned. The use must have persisted on less prominent buildings for which there were no detailed building accounts. This is confirmed by the English settlers in New England who adopted shingling for all types of buildings. There they were sawn in random widths from 2½ to 14in and were about 16in long (60-350mm x 400mm), made from cedar, cypress and redwood.[16]

Innocent also comments on the confusion surrounding the use of the word 'sclats' or slates to refer to timber, stone or ceramic elements. The word 'slats' is also used both for timber and stone slates. The forms used for shingles in Scandinavia are in part repeated in slate and tile making. The plain-ended type is universal and is the standard type for blue slates, grey slates and plain-tiles. Scalloped ends are found in decorative blue-slate and plain-tile work, as are the lancet and straight-tailed types. The earliest Roman roof tiles found in England are pear-shaped, having a scalloped tail and a truncated point above the nail hole. Slates of this type are still produced in quarries near Bergen, Norway.

The role of shingles is far from definite, since most of the evidence is based on confused nomenclature; visual representations that may show either slate, tile or shingles; and a lack of physical evidence in the form of early slate quarries or archaeological evidence from early brick works. But the most compelling piece of evidence is an account of the removal of shingles from the roof of the Canongate Tolbooth, Edinburgh (1591), in the late nineteenth century and their replacement with slates.[17] This was an important building, one of the earliest stone buildings in Canongate, still shingled about 300 years after its first construction.

John Alexander Smith, who was vice president of the Society of Antiquaries of Scotland in 1871, described his initial surprise in the following terms:

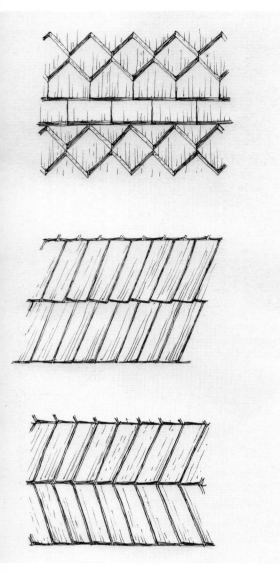

Examples of decorative shingle patterns from Austria.
(BRUCE WALKER)

Some years ago when walking with a friend down the Cannongate [sic], *on a bright sunny day, I made a discovery which rather astonished me; the sun was shining brightly, as we passed, on the picturesque roofs of the turrets and tower of the Old Tolbooth, and from its rich brown colour and general appearance, I saw that it was not covered with slates, but with wooden shingles; and my friend, who was familiar with shingled roofed church towers in Berkshire, agreed with me on this opinion. The fact was a new one to me, though it may have been known to others, and must have been well known at least to the workmen who from time to time would require to repair the roof. I looked into the various published works which gave details of the antiquities of Edinburgh and the adjoining burgh of Cannongate; but though some gave short, and others larger accounts of the Tolbooth, none that I could discover made the slightest reference to the fact of its shingled roof.*

In the course of this winter, I happened to notice various planks and scaffolding projecting around the eaves of the old building, and on making closer inspection, I found that it had been undergoing a thorough repair; but I was startled to find the shingled roof had altogether disappeared, and that it was now newly covered with small blue slates.

The man superintending the work was Andrew Slater and Smith discovered that he still had some of the shingles in his possession. He continues:

At my request he sought out various good shingles, which are all of oak, and fixed them in order on a board, sending me also some separate ones; these I have now much pleasure in presenting, in Mr Slater's name, to the Museum. The shingles measure about one foot in length, by three to five inches in breadth, and scarcely half an inch in thickness, and the ribbed and furrowed appearance of the exposed or lower extremity of each, shows the long period of time during which they have borne the varying weather of our northern climate.[18]

Canongate Tolbooth, Edinburgh, from south east, 1872.
(SOCIETY OF ANTIQUARIES OF SCOTLAND)

Dorothy Kidd of the National Museums of Scotland has located the shingle panel described above, which is shown in the accompanying illustration Smith goes on to trace some of the early references to shingles: 'They were used, as I have shown, in Anglo Saxon times, and have never since been wholly laid aside, being more easily obtained, where wood was plentiful, than tiles or slates ....'

We now need researchers to be on the lookout for further references, particularly descriptions of late changes or demolitions where the difference between slates, tiles and shingles is likely to be highlighted. Early estate records for the Aberfoyle and Dunkeld areas might also shed light on the production of shingles in these areas in periods before the slate quarries were fully established, and may show whether there was any overlap between the production of shingles and slates. However, in the author's opinion there has been too great a concentration on the Scottish slate industry, which even at the height of its production could not keep Welsh slate from gaining a substantial market in Scotland, and insufficient attention paid to this highly decorative alternative.

Panel made up from shingles taken from the Canongate Tolbooth, 1871.
(BRUCE WALKER)

Stone: Conservation of Fabric versus Conservation of Design

Bob Heath

All buildings are different: all suffer in different ways. Each building and its repair requires the establishment of a philosophy of approach before specifications are drawn up. There are many variables to be taken into account, but the major factors are: historical importance of design and/or fabric; restricting damage of original fabric; final composition and appearance; and cost versus life expectancy.

In recent years the trend for repair of stonework has been to cut out defective stones and indent new. Fortunately there has been a decrease in the use of gauged mortar repairs – which have a limited life and a deleterious effect on the fabric that they are supposed to help. The implication of indenting is that, for each stone cut out, part of the original historic fabric ends up in a skip. However, in order to keep the architectural continuity of the original design, it may be necessary to replace mouldings or a carving. And here we have the basic dilemma: which is to be conserved, the fabric or the design?

The line often taken is that classical-style architecture requires to be crisp and therefore stone renewal takes place – we can also quite often put a name to the designer. Ancient monuments, however, have usually weathered for a great number of years and have lost the original arrises and fine detail, and we are less likely to know the designer and their design philosophy. The usual approach to conservation of such structures is to treat each stone as a historic document to be protected as it is. Of course, the reality is that the majority of most standing ancient monuments were originally designed with sharp arrises and with as strong an eye for composition as classical buildings. There is no single correct approach and that is why each building requires its own philosophy, illustrated in the following examples.

The ancient monuments on Preston Island comprise Beam Engine House, an accommodation block and salt pans. They are in a highly exposed position, approximately one mile into the Firth of Forth, and this exposure has eroded the stone in the structures to the extent that collapse had occurred in the past and was certainly imminent in their future. The need was to stabilise the build structurally and then to consolidate the masonry to withstand the weather. This had to be achieved with a repair which would not accelerate weathering in the delicate original work, but would at the same time be identifiable as repair work. Another aspect to the work on site was that it had to be carried out by unskilled (albeit trained on site) labour.

The method devised was in the style of a Society for the Protection of Ancient Buildings tile repair, but using compatible sandstone. This was supplied as 150mm wide by 50mm deep and of random length that could be cut using a bolster and hammer to suit the site requirements. The resulting repair consolidates the structure, will not accelerate decay in the original fabric, is visually sympathetic, and easily read as a modern intervention. Would this have been acceptable as a method of repair for Register House, Edinburgh?

The method chosen to commence repairs on Culzean Castle by the National Trust for Scotland administrator in 1963 was to cut out and indent new stone. This was the only accepted repair technique at that time. However, the stone specified (from the Springwell Quarry in Gateshead) was dense, bland and totally foreign to Ayrshire. Use of this stone has resulted in accelerated decay in the original fabric. The opportunity arose to reconsider this approach with a requirement to slow down decay to the seaward face of the castle. The first task appeared to be to identify the causes of the degeneration, evident in the form of contour scaling. The obvious reason was the exposure of the walls to the prevailing south-west, salt-laden winds. However, as is often the case, the 'obvious reason' was not the right one. Using the castle as a test case, a PhD study was undertaken by Carolyn Hayles under the supervision of Professor Brian Bluck of Glasgow University. The true reason for the decay was established as the degeneration of volcanic clays laid down in the original sandstone (changing from solid to liquid when exposed to the atmosphere). As the change takes place, the clays expand and the stone literally bursts along a line back from the face at the depth of moisture penetration. In the case of Culzean, this was approximately 25mm deep, resulting in that depth of face detaching (ie a contour scale).

The philosophy of approach was to remove scaled and flaking stone along with poor cement patches from the surface of the building and to repoint as necessary. This enables the original fabric to undergo a new weathering cycle which should be at a slower rate, without moisture being held in the wall and prevented from drying by the scales, as previously. Defective structural and weathering features such as lintels, cills, cornice and string courses were replaced in new stone. The result still conveys Adam's architecture, albeit with softer detailing, and the building should now be in a sound weathering condition for at least 100 years.

Allison House: poor and past repair by pointing, decay has been caused in this stonework and good original bedding. The result is a high level of dangerous patches in the wall.
(BOB HEATH)

Preston Island accommodation block: an example of structural consolidation of a ruin using the contemporary SPAB (Society for the Protection of Ancient Buildings) tile repair technique, but here with compatible sandstone.
(BOB HEATH)

A similar approach was taken at Cannonball House, Castlehill, Edinburgh, where massive amounts of cement patching and pointing were removed from a basically rubble building. The result is like grandma's knitted jumper – a bit woolly with a few dropped stitches, but still keeping you warm and dry. Would the National Trust for Scotland have allowed this approach to be taken for the garden front of the castle?

Sometimes it is necessary to consolidate stonework without actually doing repairs to it, as in the case of the Camellia House at Culzean. This building, a beautiful ruin, was structurally undermined to the extent that a tight-jointed mullion fell out in storm conditions and another twisted through 90 degrees. The stonework needed to be tied together in some manner. This could have been achieved by introducing exposed steel or stainless steel bands or strappings, and the whole left as a consolidated ruin. However, the philosophy of approach and action taken was to re-roof the building in a contemporary and sympathetic manner using the introduced work to support the original masonry. From a distance it looks similar to the original design, but close to it is obviously a twentieth-century intervention. The end result adds to both the history and enjoyment of the building and allows it to be used. Would this approach be suitable for a medieval abbey in the Borders?

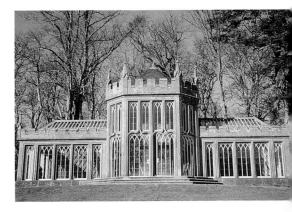

Camellia House, Culzean, demonstrates conservation of a building's fabric by re-roofing and reglazing. These added necessary structural support to the fragile stonework.
(BOB HEATH)

With the Pagoda at Culzean, as with the Camellia House, we were faced with the problem of consolidating a ruin and in this case protecting it from certain vandalism. Many approaches were considered, such as consolidating and repairing on an annual basis, enclosing it in a glazed box or, dare it be said, restoration. The approach was similar to that for the Camellia House, but incorporated a little more humour. The importance of this building in the landscape lies in its position in the vista from the Swan Pond. It now looks much as it would have appeared in April 1814 when it was completed. Its original use was a house for exotic birds and monkeys, as well as a teahouse, and it was known in the early twentieth century as the monkey house. Using this base we introduced contemporary details to replace long-lost and forgotten work, hence the monkey-tail balustrading and the monkey sitting atop the building as a weather vane. These are, of course, side issues – the most important aspect for the protection of original fabric was the reintroduction of lime harling. How much fun should you be allowed to have with historic buildings?

The Pagoda at Culzean: conservation by reconstruction, making a total ruin into a good building with contemporary detailing.
(BOB HEATH)

In the restoration and consolidation of buildings, all tools and approaches which will ultimately benefit the building must be considered, including covering the stonework for its protection. Consideration must be given to replastering buildings, even where the plaster has been missing for 200 years, as on the west side of George Square in Edinburgh. The only true way of protecting the stonework (which was never meant to be exposed) is to cover it up to prevent its erosion and decay. It must also be considered as a contemporary intervention where original ashlar work has decayed to the state of requiring protection. It is a reversible repair after all, and has proved successful in the case of the House of Gray, Dundee, and in the High Street, Kirkcaldy. Would it be an acceptable method for a Gothic building?

Stone repair, like indenting, must not be undertaken lightly; for rarely are we able to replace stonework like-for-like, since original sources of material are often inaccessible and even original quarries change over time. Doddington sandstone, for instance, was renowned for its pink hue but is now buff-coloured and Dunhouse grey sandstone is now brown. However, they could return to their original colours tomorrow – it is simply not very predictable.

In conclusion, do not accept what is presented as acceptable philosophy for repair. Always question before constructing your approach and always do what is best for the building. You and your clients are but temporary guardians.

Culross Palace, recently given a new 'breathable' lime harl with coloured lime wash finish.
(NTS)

Mortars, Renders and Plasters

Pat Gibbons

The title of this book is interesting. *Caring for the Scottish Home* perhaps implies a degree of loving care? Not only are these buildings sculptural objects in the landscape or components of a distinctive townscape, but they are our homes – places where we eat and sleep, relax and work. Although we might sometimes be prepared to tolerate the occasional idiosyncrasy on the grounds of age or character, on the whole we expect modern standards of comfort and performance. Given appropriate understanding and maintenance there is no reason why this should not be possible.

In order to care for traditionally constructed buildings – to exclude the weather and maintain comfortable living conditions, and to retain their unique character – it is important to appreciate the way in which they work. You will be familiar with the analogy of a Goretex or Harris tweed jacket versus a plastic macintosh. One manages moisture levels by allowing 'breathing' and evaporation; the other excludes all water (provided there are no holes) but causes unpleasant sweating. In the same way, the technology of traditional building construction is very different from that of most modern buildings. Traditionally constructed buildings tend to rely on an ability to handle and manage moisture within the building fabric. Modern construction aims to totally exclude moisture.

Traditional masonry structures were built as mass construction, generally without the application of impermeable finishes, and without the incorporation of membranes and damp-proof courses which modern construction employs. Most masonry materials and their bedding mortars are porous and permeable to some degree. This improves their ability to take in and release water and water vapour. In addition, many buildings were originally finished with a coating of lime harl. Lime mortar used as an external coating material will exclude a certain amount of water but remains essentially porous and permeable. Excess water taken into the wall finish will evaporate again, when conditions allow. In a continuous cycle of wetting and drying, rainwater is retained mainly in the outer part of the wall; the lime finishing layer minimising water movement or retention, and associated deterioration, in the masonry itself. In severe conditions, a mass of lime in the core of the wall can 'mop up' penetrating water and minimise the risk of penetration to the interior.

Another difference occurs in the way traditional and modern buildings react to movement. All buildings flex in response to thermal and seasonal changes, or even to ground movement. Traditional mass-wall construction handles this movement through a degree of overall flexibility, brought about by the use of numerous small units (stones or bricks) set in a relatively soft mortar. Modern rigid construction requires the incorporation of specially designed 'movement joints' at intervals in the construction. The characteristics of breathability and flexibility are also important, and the availability of compatible, breathable materials is critical to the well-being of traditional houses.

The most effective methods of repair and maintenance will almost invariably involve the use of materials and techniques employed in the original construction of the house. These might include clay or earth mortars or traditional lime mortars, all of which are more permeable and more flexible than cement mortars and contain fewer potentially damaging salts. They also look better – it is simply not possible to achieve an authentic appearance without the use of authentic materials. The imposition of hard grey cement in a rigid pattern of jointing, emphasising each individual stone, or the application of a brittle cementitious render finished with a modern paint system, is alien to the expected softness and warmth in appearance of a traditional masonry or harled wall. As well as altering the appearance of traditional buildings, cement-based mortars will also alter their performance, almost invariably for the worse.

Damage to traditional masonry buildings as a result of inappropriate repairs is now a widespread problem. The search for permanent 'maintenance free' treatments during the second half of the twentieth century has left a legacy of accelerated decay in stone surfaces and has caused significant problems of dampness and timber decay. In selecting materials for the repair or replacement of mortars, renders and plasters, we should be considering the range of materials traditionally used. This will include earth and clay mortars, with or without various additives; lime mortars of various types; mixes containing combinations of earth and lime; and, perhaps, some of the later, harder setting, mortars.

Although lime seems to have been known as a building material for over 7000 years, its use in domestic buildings in Scotland is much more recent. Early mortars were most likely to have been earth-based materials, perhaps reinforced with vegetable fibres such as straw, or in the form of turf. Although lime mortars were used in many of the grander buildings from medieval times, they may not have been in common domestic use much before the seventeenth century. Once the use of lime for agricultural improvements was appreciated, it also quickly became accepted as a common building material. This took the form of construction mortar and mortar for external coatings and internal finishing, and for use as paint; and a parallel tradition developed alongside that of earth-based mortars. Lime-based mortars have been widely used from the late seventeenth century, both in urban development and in the steadings and cottages of agricultural improvements.

During the eighteenth and nineteenth centuries the use of lime mortars of various types became the norm, alongside a gradually declining local use of earthen mortars. In the early twentieth century an increasing use of cementitious materials occurred and by the mid twentieth century their use was almost universal. Realisation of the damage that can be caused to traditional buildings by the use of excessively hard and impermeable mortars has resulted in the recent reintroduction of lime mortars for repair and conservation.

Earth-based materials were normally extracted locally, tempered by working and sometimes reinforced with vegetable fibres. Earth or loam might be used with or without the addition of sand or gravel. Clay would normally be combined with a coarse sand or gravel filler. Pointing up with lime mortar where this was available might protect joints in earth-bound masonry walls, or the external wall surface might be coated with a clay or lime-based render, protected by a coating of limewash. Internally, wall surfaces might be plastered with clay, with or without a

Drum Castle, Old Tower (13th century), with remnants of early lime harl on rounded corners. This harl is only a few millimetres thick yet has proven to be durable. (NTS)

Redundant lime kiln at Boyne Bay on the Moray coast.
(NTS)

limewash finish or perhaps coated in a lime plaster. Other special mortars, such as clay/cowdung mixes, could be utilised for chimney linings or for external weather-proof finishes. Where lime was available, there is evidence for mortars and plasters containing clay/lime mixes. Clay-based building materials are excellent for managing moisture and humidity levels in buildings and, provided they are maintained and are not compromised by the introduction of impermeable materials (such as cement and plastic paints), they will continue to function efficiently.

It is reasonable to assume that local sources of lime were utilised where available, although there is evidence that these were being supplemented by the output of larger scale limeworks by the late eighteenth century. Within the complex geology of Scotland, limestone deposits are variable, giving rise, historically, to locally varied mortars, as well as providing a rich source of potential types and strengths in lime mortars throughout the country. The majority of Scottish limestones produced feebly hydraulic lime mortars; others were non-hydraulic or strongly hydraulic. Even within clearly defined geological areas, considerable variation occurred in the type and strength of limes produced.

Lime production involves burning or heating limestone to convert calcium carbonate to calcium oxide with the driving off of carbon dioxide. This process is normally carried out in a lime kiln, and the remains of many old kilns survive throughout Scotland. After burning, the calcium oxide (or 'quicklime') is converted to lime (calcium hydroxide) by combining with water in a process known as 'slaking'. Lime mortars comprise a mixture of lime with a sand filler and, depending on their chemical composition and method of production, harden either simply by reabsorbing carbon dioxide, or in a more complex process that also involves chemical hardening.

As explained above, the use of matching or compatible materials in repair and maintenance work is important. Earth and clay-based materials for repair or maintenance are generally obtained locally, although some commercial supplies are starting to become available. Although, unfortunately, lime is not produced commercially in Scotland at present, this could change in the foreseeable future. In the meantime, supplies of English and continental limes are available from Scottish outlets. Lime comes in a wide range of different properties and strengths, enabling the characteristics of surviving historic materials to be matched and providing new materials suitable for a variety of applications and exposure conditions. Current programmes of research are investigating the influence of lime burning and production methods on performance, with the objective of reintroducing some of the complex materials found in surviving historic mortars.

Lime mortars, whether for use in bedding or pointing masonry, or for external or internal coatings, are made by combining lime and a filler such as coarse sand. Fine sands might be used in finishing plaster and mortar for repointing fine ashlar joints. The softer setting mortars (non-hydraulic mortars) can be made up in advance of use and are available, ready made, from suppliers of traditional mortars. Harder setting mortars (hydraulic mortars) must be made up shortly before use and are normally made on site by combining dry bagged hydraulic lime with sand and water. The selection of a mortar type appropriate to the job and the location is important.

Before undertaking a programme of repair works, careful investigation is required to establish the original materials and to understand the dynamics of the building. Investigation and understanding of the architectural development of a historic building has long been accepted as the norm, whilst current practice also puts emphasis on the social and 'cultural' importance. Alongside these concerns, an understanding of the technology of the building is essential if repairs are to be effective. Effective repair of traditional buildings relies on a holistic approach, taking account of the overall behaviour pattern of the building in its local environment.

Traditional permeable mortar materials require an overall environment of good building repair to maintain their decorative and protective qualities. Where other building elements are not adequately maintained, the performance of traditional mortar materials, whether in the form of coatings or jointing mortar, will be compromised. Once the dynamics of building performance, including patterns of decay, have been understood, a strategy for conservation or repair can be developed. In the past, decay of a lime harling, for example, has too often been regarded as an underlying failure of the material. This has led to its replacement by a cementitious coating without investigation and resolution of the causal factors of failure, such as inadequate maintenance of rainwater goods or inappropriate building details.

Repairs might be required to jointing mortar, due either to gradual deterioration over many years, or, for example, to lack of maintenance of rainwater goods. Reinstatement of lime mortar jointing might also be required following inappropriate cementitious pointing, where the hard mortar has encouraged accelerated decay in the stones themselves.

External lime coatings can survive for several hundred years given a favourable environment and appropriate building maintenance, but more frequent renewal is often necessary. Removal of cementitious coatings and the reinstatement of lime finishes is a common requirement. It will often be found that cement renders have trapped moisture in the wall fabric, leading to dampness, timber decay and, of course, to stone decay associated with the presence of sulphates or other salts behind the cement render.

Internal lime plaster finishes normally survive for very long periods, except where decay or movement of timber substrates causes mechanical failure. Most internal plasters before the early twentieth century are lime-based, although many from the early eighteenth century onwards will also have a small gypsum content. The behaviour and properties of modern, wholly gypsum-based plasters are significantly different from those of lime-based plasters and these newer materials should never be used to patch traditional plasterwork.

Techniques for use of traditional mortars, renders and plasters require skills which have to be learned by practice. Major repair or reinstatement of earth and clay-based mortars should only be tackled by workers familiar with the materials and their properties. Similarly, the repair and reinstatement of lime-based materials requires an informed approach.

Unfortunately modern lime materials and skills do not, at present, always achieve the longevity of many traditional applications – but we are working on the problem! The successful use of new lime mortars depends both on the materials themselves and on appropriate conditions and techniques of use. Skilled craftsmen and good site practice are of fundamental importance, as is the availability of high-quality, durable lime mortars. The former can be addressed by training and the latter by research and development work, such as that currently underway at the new experimental lime kiln at Charlestown in Fife.

The life expectancy of traditional permeable mortar materials can be directly influenced by any of the following: availability and selection of an appropriate good quality mortar; techniques and quality of workmanship (including effective

Detail of Brodie Castle, Forres. Lime harling, left; cement harling, right.
(NTS)

preparation of materials and backgrounds, removal of vegetation, careful and knowledgeable application and appropriate curing after application, usually involving some form of protection); building detailing; local environmental conditions; and the maintenance regime.

Traditional masonry buildings require regular routine maintenance as well as long-term maintenance. For many building owners a simple routine of checking, and 'do-it-yourself' or local tradesman care on the level of housekeeping maintenance, would minimise the need for large-scale repairs. At this level special skills are not essential – a commonsense approach and a basic understanding of the building and its materials are all that is required. For those owners who do not feel sufficiently confident to tackle basic housekeeping maintenance, help is at hand. This comes in the form of short courses or one-day workshops run by the National Trust for Scotland, the Society for the Protection of Ancient Buildings, the Building Limes Forum, the Scottish Lime Centre Trust, and others. Published guidance is also available from Historic Scotland in the form of their Technical Advice Notes.

A good maintenance strategy will focus attention both on mortar materials themselves and on other aspects of a building's fabric. Along with the routine tasks of keeping rhones clear of debris, checking and fixing loose slates, and checking ground drainage, the touching up of any minor degradation of finishes should be normal practice. The lifespan of traditional external finishes will be significantly enhanced by prompt attention to minor defects. Monitoring of rainwater disposal systems – a basic requirement for any type of building – is critical to the performance of traditional mortar finishes.

Maintenance requirements for buildings containing earth and clay involve regular inspection and prompt making good of minor defects by patching in with matching materials. No alien materials should be introduced and the use of cement-based mortars or modern paint systems must be totally avoided. Earth-based materials rely on an appropriate level of moisture – if they become totally dried out they will crumble and disintegrate. On the other hand, too much water will also cause failure.

Where buildings have a limewash finish, routine 'housekeeping' maintenance on a domestic scale can be undertaken very simply by brush application of limewash to minor defects if and when necessary. Limewash can be kept in a re-sealing container for this purpose. Similarly, minor degradation of harling can be patched in by hand, using a matching ready-mixed lime mortar kept for this purpose. (Pre-mixed basic lime mortars may be stored for long periods of time.)

Traditional domestic buildings almost invariably contain permeable mortars, either lime-based or, less frequently, earth-based. These may be in the form of construction mortars, external coatings or internal plastered finishes. Effective performance of these mortars is critical to the overall well-being of a building and, conversely, effective maintenance of a building is required to ensure the performance of mortars. A holistic approach is required to the care of traditional buildings. Major repair or reinstatement of traditional mortar materials requires selection of appropriate materials and informed and skilled workers; but with a little understanding, common sense and enthusiasm, owners or local tradesmen can tackle routine housekeeping maintenance which, performed regularly, will significantly reduce the need for major repairs.

Timber

Ben Tindall

The building material most often associated with Scottish architecture is stone. People tend to think of picturesque crofts, sturdy farms, elegant terraces, and great castles in granite, slate and sandstone. Timber is not generally thought of as a basic material of the house, but this is one of many misconceptions about it. In fact, most houses in Scotland, traditional or modern, are just a thin skin of masonry, brick or concrete, filled in with softer timber from top to bottom. Timber makes up the majority of the construction of a house and is a distinguishing feature of Scottish building. It is not necessarily the only way to build, but in England and on the Continent, where timber is in greater supply, far more timber is used.

Timber is a manageable and adaptable material which can therefore be used in many ways. There are three different kinds of timber used in construction work: green, seasoned and processed. The qualities, skills, specification and treatment for each type are completely different. Green timber is the material that has been used for vernacular buildings and furniture for thousands of years; it is still used in 'less developed' countries throughout the world for self-build. The moisture in green timber means that much of it is worked by splitting, with the axe, side axe and adze. This is a remarkably effective and very efficient use of human and renewable energy. Regrettably, very little green timber is used today. There is lots of information on the subject, the majority of it deriving from Freddie Charles.[1]

Seasoned timber is, by definition, cut, and accounts for the vast majority of timber used in Scotland today. Seasoning reduces the amount of woodworm, warping, twisting and wastage at later stages of the construction process. The greater part of seasoned timber is softwood. Timber with sapwood, however, which is more prone to rot, is no longer rejected. Instead, all structural timber is now treated with chemicals. Likewise, timber with knots is also now used; in fact Scandinavia exports it for use in Scotland. Seasoned timber is worked with the saw and the plane, a more energy-consuming operation than with axe and adze. Once worked, however, the material is relatively stable and easy to fix. Getting a matching timber for repair work is extremely difficult; second-hand or salvaged material is likely to be the closest match.

Finally, processed timber is the contemporary high-embodied energy solution to some of the problems created by over-exploitation of forests and the resultant timber shortage. Processed timber uses glue to hold together the waste of converting timber. The most artificial timber material is MDF (medium density fibreboard), which is absolutely without character. Some forms of constructing beams and posts use relatively little glue and are excellent ways of using forest thinnings.

The properties of each species of tree used for constructional timbers vary greatly. Among both the redwoods (pines) and the whitewoods (spruces and firs) there is a vast range of different species. Traditionally, most of the timber used for building was of exceptional quality, selected in the forest to be worth the transport to market, down great river basins. Most of it was also from slow-grown virgin forests in Norway, the Baltic basin or North America. Some timber, of course, was indigenous, for example the Scots Pine which was floated down the Spey. Much of this was used for shipbuilding, and some for water pipes[2] rather than house construction.

Timber makes up a major proportion of the construction of Scottish houses. The Vaults, Leith, Edinburgh.
(BENJAMIN TINDALL ARCHITECTS)

Historically, most houses were self-built and made with 'green' unseasoned timber. Strath Kanaird, Ross-shire.
(BENJAMIN TINDALL ARCHITECTS)

The key features in the understanding of the use of all kinds of timber are those for any organic material: movement, breathing and ventilation. With good ventilation, timber can last almost indefinitely. It expands and shrinks with the amount of moisture in the surrounding atmosphere. However carefully seasoned the timber might be, nothing will prevent this and, of course, it moves more across the grain than along it. Careful detailing and specification are all that is required to ensure long life.

The great enemy of timber is rot, especially in a damp climate. Without the provision for a building to breathe, or without proper ventilation, moisture can reach levels similar to those that might be expected on a forest floor, allowing natural decay mechanisms to set in. Damp is a particular problem in Scotland, especially where the masonry is impermeable, for example in buildings made of whin or granite, and where the rainfall and wind speeds are high.[3] Dry-rot 'attacks' should never be a surprise. They are always due to high moisture levels and are nearly always the result of simple neglect. Woodworm, likewise, is nearly always the result of excessive moisture: woodworm do not like eating dry timber.

The solution to rot 'problems' is to bring the moisture content of the timber and its environment down to a safe level. 'Free' advice from 'specialist' rot companies is rarely impartial or independent, and their reports and guarantees are seldom worth much.[4] Indeed, treatments applied can be contrary to the 'Control of Substances Hazardous to Health' regulations. The use of chemicals, which in reality means poisons, is seldom a fundamental or satisfactory solution to rot problems. The only time to consider their use is where drying out cannot be arranged quickly enough and the new timber is liable to be affected by damp for a short period of, for example, two years. The requirement of Building Societies in this regard should be resisted, perhaps with the help of the Society for the Protection of Ancient Buildings (SPAB) leaflet *Is Timber Treatment Always Necessary?*[5]

Rot is only a problem when the structure or the surface finish of timber has been affected. An intelligent solution might accept some dead rot, as long as the source of moisture has been fundamentally dealt with and it cannot become a danger. The supply of intelligent solutions is short, but can be found in, for example, Brian Ridout's book, *Timber Decay in Buildings* (commissioned by Historic Scotland and English Heritage), which will not make happy reading for many rot treatment companies.

In addition to the problems caused by moisture in timber, the sun is also a threat, destroying the surface fibres, turning them silver grey through the action of ultraviolet radiation. Internally, timber is turned dark by the action of infra-red radiation. The treatment, if desired, is to protect the timber with a suitable protective coating of paint.

Finally, of course, there is fire. Unlike steel, which becomes plastic at high temperatures, timber burns at a slow rate because it is an excellent insulating material, keeping its structural integrity for a considerable time. The treatment of timber against fire is a secondary matter, but, of course, it is better that fire should be prevented in the first place and Historic Scotland's recent Technical Advice Notes give excellent guidance.[6] Timber can be treated to make it more fire resistant, but most treatments alter its appearance.

Traditionally, carpenters are responsible for timber which is used structurally and the definition of a carpenter is someone who works timber without a plane. Historically, it was carpenters who carried out the functions of engineers, builders and architects for a large number of ordinary buildings.

Roofs made of green timber are mostly vernacular and are few in Scotland, Stirling Castle's Great Hall new roof being a spectacular exception. Timber is, however, making a comeback. Green timber shrinks an enormous amount during and just after construction, but seldom does the natural cracking have any structural effect. To repair such roofs with seasoned wood is to use the wrong material. Freddie Charles' book and the SPAB leaflet *The Repair of Timber Frames and Roofs* both give excellent advice.[7]

Most roofs have been made from seasoned timber.[8] In Scotland most domestic roofs are in the form of simple 'couples'. Until fairly recently the sizing of the timbers had been based on empirical knowledge, using relatively unsophisticated nail fixings. The detailed design of many Victorian roofs, especially of the 'baronial' style, was done without consideration of their vulnerability to water penetration, so lack of maintenance may lead to dry rot in confined spaces. The repairs carried out by so-called specialists sometimes become the weakest points of the roof. Pieces of wood are often simply crudely bolted onto existing rafters, often without the use of shear connectors. Contemporary trussed rafter roofs use less timber, but do not have the same generous margin for error and neglect, or usable roof-spaces.

Both green and seasoned timbers have been used in solid masonry walls to a large degree. Bonding timbers have been used to hold masonry together while the weak lime mortar sets. These built-in timbers are all very vulnerable with regard to the inevitable damp in the outside wall, and sometimes provide a perfect network for rot to surround an entire building.

Similarly, many masonry walls rely on timber 'safe' lintels over windows and doors. Where they have lost structural integrity they are generally easily replaced with same-sized concrete pre-cast lintels. Timber grounds are usually built in to provide the fixings required for strapping, lath and plaster, and finishings generally. Although 'dooks' are often rotten,[9] the strapping usually remains structurally sound and can be kept, with new metal fixings. The amount of timber used for strapping in a traditionally built masonry house is similar to that used in a modern timber-framed house. As modern timber-framed construction has not yet stood the test of time, it is, as yet, unknown what will affect it most.

For floors, timber is the norm. Most floors are of a simple joist construction, often traditionally filled with deafening to provide effective sound insulation. Sometimes the floors are of principal and secondary beams. Defects in these floors can be hard to analyse, often requiring a good engineer. The joist or beam-ends are frequently built into the damp outer masonry skin and consequently have decayed. Unfortunately the repairs carried out by 'specialist' rot companies are usually very crude and destroy a lot of original sound material. Occasionally the repaired timbers are wrapped in polythene or the equivalent, but no wrapping can influence the dampness of the environment the timber is placed in.

The real answer may well be to provide appropriate brackets. There are many different ingenious and sensitive ways of strengthening beams. The SPAB leaflet on the subject is an excellent introduction, making it clear that every situation needs to be considered on its own merits.[10] Generally, timber floors at ground level are of a suspended construction, with a ventilated solum. Wherever the ventilation is inadequate, moisture levels are likely to rise to levels where rot is inevitable. The real solution is to introduce ventilation.

High quality native Scots pine. Rothiemurchus, Inverness-shire.
(BENJAMIN TINDALL ARCHITECTS)

Traditional Materials and Repair

Chippings, for conversion into chipboard. Oregon, United States of America.
(BENJAMIN TINDALL ARCHITECTS)

Moisture is the main enemy of timber, usually caused by simple neglect. Doune Mill, Ross-shire.
(BENJAMIN TINDALL ARCHITECTS)

Tongued-and-grooved floorboards were introduced in the 1820s.[11] Any older floor should be carefully preserved and treated with the greatest of care. The greatest danger to floors is electricians and heating engineers, both unqualified to work with timber. Joiners should always lift floorboards. Normally whole boards should be lifted, and replaced with screws rather than nailing them down, which seldom lasts long. Squeaky boards can be cured with the application of talcum powder, which does not stain or expand the wood.

In addition, fashion causes great damage. For example, sanding and polyurethaning timber rarely produces the beautiful results intended. The sanding destroys the patina of age and exposes the nail-holes that have held down carpets and coverings, knots and other defects. The hard finish on top of the floor soon breaks down as the timber underneath is softer, leading to a cycle of yet more sanding and the eventual replacement of the floor itself. If it is considered essential that the timber should be sealed, which is not the norm in Scandinavia, and was not common in Britain before the nineteenth century, a wax should be used instead of a varnish.

For windows, timber has proved to be a highly durable as well as beautiful material. Early windows were made of oak and, until the 1950s, selected redwood. Since then, unselected timber, with a great deal of sapwood, has been used, and it has proved to be a false economy. These windows have not lasted more than a few years. In far too many cases this has given all timber windows a bad reputation, despite the obvious existence of 200 year-old timber windows. Unlike steel, aluminium or plastic, timber windows can be easily repaired, not with plastic inserts, but with the replacement of the timber parting bead and other simple works. Repairs with traditional materials, rather than resins, tend to be reversible and sustainable. Timber windows can provide additional sound and heat insulation with the use of secondary glazing, again best done in timber frames.

The main hazards to timber doors are fire regulations and fashion. Numerous houses have been ruined by the replacement of original doors. There are no statistics that demonstrate that the fire resistance of timber doors is a major problem. Nonetheless, the concept of fire doors is deeply enshrined in fire safety regulations. The concept seems to be based on the idea that doors need to resist a fiery furnace being dropped from the ceiling above. But it has long been recognised that smoke is a much greater danger.[12] Of fires that spread out of control, 85% spread through open doors whatever their construction. The use of self-closers and improvements to doorframes are the practical ways of making an escape route safe in these respects, and can be non-destructively tested with a cold smoke test. To satisfy fire regulations, intumescent paints and veneers have to be used to increase the thermal insulation properties of a door, along with strengthening any weak joints.

Dipping and stripping doors to expose the timber is, thankfully, going out of fashion. Caustic baths used in the process weaken joints made with animal glues, as well as seriously affecting the timber itself. If the timber of a door was originally intended to be exposed, the careful removing of finishes with the use of hot air guns and caustic pastes is much to be preferred. It was rare, however, that softwoods were originally intended to be seen. In fact, Robert Lorimer even used mahogany for door facings precisely because it gave a better finish for painting. Fashion, of course, is an entirely natural force, but the replacement of solid doors with flimsy ones is not advisable. In Conservation Areas and for Listed Buildings, consent is required for such modifications, and should generally be refused.

Historically, panelling was a very practical as well as attractive way of finishing walls in the houses of the wealthy, making them warm and dry. Panels were nearly always of pine and intended to be painted. In earlier times, panelling was like furniture or a tapestry and travelled with the household from property to property. Pictures and candleholders were often nailed to the panelling without particular regard to the panels. Panelling repairs are difficult to carry out piecemeal. It is usually easiest to take down a complete section, take it apart, repair or replace the minimum necessary, rebuild and re-fix.

The painted timber ceilings of Scotland, while now rare, were a relatively common feature in the sixteenth century in churches and wealthy homes, reflecting foreign tastes. Scotland after the Reformation was not quite the dour and sober place some people imagine.[13] In Aberdeen such timber ceilings are visible at St Machar's Cathedral and Provost Skene's House. The care and repair of painted ceilings is for the professional conservationists.

Timber hand-railing is a craft that has been sadly abused, requiring too much mathematical application for most people. It is not something that can be 'done by eye'.[14] Sweet curves are made by cutting the shape out of large pieces of timber to suit the mathematics concerned. The jointing, and sometimes veneering, of the rail is a simpler matter once the geometry is right. The number of craftspeople capable of undertaking such work is unfortunately limited; but they are limited by low demand for such work. The cost is, of course, high, but so is the pleasure, a factor which applies to all skills.

SPAB, of which I am currently Convenor, upholds the essential philosophy of 'repair not restore'. SPAB believes that it is impossible to recreate the past, and that its value is best maintained by careful repair. Indeed, a solid repair by skilled craftsmen enhances a property's financial as well as cultural value. Our philosophy is the foundation of all modern conservation charters around the world. It is also the basis of the many excellent leaflets published by SPAB to assist the public with advice on the conservation of their properties.

In Scotland we have held events in various parts of the country on Scottish issues as varied as penetrating damp in Argyll and the loss of timber windows in Montrose. SPAB believes that thorough survey and analysis are the keys to good repair, along with understanding the structure of the property, proper site control, imagination and creativity. Finally, SPAB in Scotland (SPABiS) has a committee with a number of good engineers, surveyors and craftsmen, and is very willing to point people in the right direction for detailed practical and professional advice on all issues of conservation, not just timber.

Repairs by 'specialist' rot companies can leave a lot to be desired. Here the use of under-sized timbers bolted together without toothed washers was worse than the original defect. Great King Street, Edinburgh. (BENJAMIN TINDALL ARCHITECTS)

Panelling provides warmth as well as beauty, but when affected by neglect requires skilled repair. Normally the joints have to be carefully dismantled. (HERMITS & TERMITS, EDINBURGH)

Traditional Paint

Peter Maitland Hood

There are considerable differences between traditional paints and the paints generally used today. For example, the black gloss often applied to iron railings originated long ago as a mixture of tar oil, asphaltum and natural resin. This remained flexible and waterproof and would hardly have split and peeled back to

19th-century paint over 17th-century tempera decoration in the Muses Room at Crathes Castle, Kincardineshire.
(NTS)

expose the iron, like the equivalent black gloss today. Traditional black paint was used primarily for its function and often the colour was consequential. Where paint was decorative, it usually involved recognisable materials. Its production was in the hands of the user.

Paint is a self-drying liquid applied as a coating for protective and decorative purposes, or for indication, as on postboxes or signs. The word itself, from Old French *peint,* is ultimately derived from Latin. It was originally used to describe coatings with an oil medium as distinct from the types involving water as a medium. The term 'paint' essentially described an oil-bound coating as distinct from traditional distemper, which is skin-glue-bound. Small amounts of boiled linseed oil were sometimes added to distemper to make it harder. In the late nineteenth century superfine oil paints, emulsified and water miscible, were developed by industrialists. The term 'oil-bound distemper' came into use for this forebear of today's emulsions, despite a ruling by the Institute of British Decorators that the term 'water paint' should be used (as distinct from the phrase 'oil paint').

The word 'traditional' derives from Latin *tradere* (deliver). It came to describe things made with knowledge: understanding or practices carried or passed down from generation to generation. Today, of course, it often only suggests something old-fashioned and therefore reliable, as a contrast to synthetic and 'modern'. 'Traditional paint' in this chapter refers to the old tradition, made following handed-down precepts.

Paint is not found in nature, though many of the ingredients are natural. It has to be made and, before the nineteenth century, house painters made their own paint. Most of the ingredients were imported and purchased from sea-trading merchants and their agents. Certain pigments were semi-precious and therefore expensive. Since the early seventeenth century colour pigments such as white lead[1] had become commercial industrial products, and oil and colour merchants offered pigments ground in oil for house painters in the early eighteenth century. It was the development of cast-iron machinery that made it possible for commercial industrialists to make revolutionary new paints based on zinc compounds[2] that were beyond the capabilities and traditional understanding of most house painters and decorators. These new paints were the forebears of today's types and, due to their zinc compound base, were hydrophobic. They therefore retained their white appearance and had a harder surface, despite repeated washing with soap and water and the bad atmosphere of places like nineteenth-century railway terminals. In such polluted locations, the white-lead paints of tradition were turned stone colour by the sulphurous smoke.[3] The new paints were promoted as having 40% better covering power and density and as being cheaper; although even their makers admitted that it was best to mix them with white-lead paint 'as a finishing coat for outside work'.

For indoor plasterwork, an emulsified version of these new zinc paints was developed as water paint, the precursor of today's emulsion paints. The traditional ingredients and production methods came to be modified by the industrialists. Speed, convenience and price, rather than the house painter's traditional precepts, became central to paint production. By the 1880s ready-prepared paints were made available and were widely distributed in a similar way to those we have today. This resulted in a break with tradition as more and more painters were required by architects and other specifiers to use these proprietary products. The new paints were essentially different to, and less responsive in nature than, those of the old tradition.

In ancient times the houses of the nobility, gentry and merchants were mainly constructed of stone and timber, whereas those of the rural, labouring class were mostly built of earth or divots. These materials are broken down by, for example, drying out, weathering and exposure to harmful light rays such as ultra-violet. Mortar and harling were therefore essential protection against the wind, but not necessarily against rainwater penetration. In Scotland's wet climate paints were always particularly useful for adding water resistance. They also provided a freshening coat of white or colour and suggested the finishes of the more costly houses in better climates. It may have been more usual than sometimes thought today for the entire fabric of more expensive houses to be finished with coats of paint, with the exception, of course, of the window glass. This overcoat masked and unified the variable shades of stones, lead sheets and timbers, yet could present the appearance of the best of their sort. Cast-based materials such as iron or plaster could be painted to suggest superior bronze or marble.

The Muses Room at Crathes Castle, detail. (NTS)

Timber was generally used for framework, roof trusses, floors, doors, windows and weatherboarding. Following the 'scorched earth' strategy that prevailed during the civil wars, there were great shortages of timber in Scotland in the seventeenth and early eighteenth centuries. It was necessary to import most timber and generally all timber, even oak, was painted. It was well known that the best lead-based paints proved the most resistant to weathering, thermal movement and physical damage, as well as inhibiting woodboring insects.

Almost inseparable from lead-based paints was the development by the Dutch of the sliding-sash window, inspired by ships' horizontally sliding casements. For the sashes, white-lead paints were essential. Most of the first sash frames in Scotland were imported from Holland, obtained by trade as 'staple goods'. Other 'staple goods' were white lead and oil. For hinges, casement frames, hooks, bracelets, bolts, knobs and knockers, people relied on wrought iron, mostly produced domestically. Whereas the best wrought iron might be thought not to need paint, rust resistance was hard to guarantee at the time. Wrought iron was therefore usually protected by lead-based oil paint, usually with some kind of hydrophobic pigment ingredient (such as tar) added.

Paint was probably first made in prehistory for painting ships and the timber frames and boardings of buildings. In composition, a traditional paint is usually made up of a pigment and a binder and thinned to make a laminated system of coats for better attachment and durability. Several thin coats came to be recognised as superior to a few thick ones and certain ingredients were recognised for imparting better drying, elasticity and binding properties. Most of the pigments were developments or synthetic simulations of discovered natural phenomena. White lead was the only known white pigment that did not become transparent in oil. It required little to bind it, so remained more durable in daylight (ultraviolet rays were otherwise destructive of the oil binder), and remained the predominant base of the most durable oil paints for thousands of years. According to Dioscordes, a ship loaded with white lead caught fire in Piraeus harbour in around 2500BC and the resultant red lead gave us a protective, self-drying primer for painting ironwork that remains the standard by which all types can be compared today.

In traditional paint the pigments were usually ground into a self-drying and hardening binder oil, with an appropriate thinner to aid application. These 'drying oils' were those that hardened by absorbing oxygen. The best was considered to be walnut oil, which makes a more durable paint with less yellow staining than others.

Poppy-seed oil was nearly as useful, but in our northern climate linseed oil remained the more economic, although it turned more yellow in the absence of light. Traditionally these drying oils were obtained by pressing them out of linen-cloth bag containers so that they were unaffected by heat, followed by filtering and long-term settlement. The oil itself formed a flexible, water-resistant film, reduced by the volume and nature of the pigment so that white-lead paints, which used to be only 20% oil, could remain water permeable.

The traditional thinner for oil paint was almost always oil of turpentine, now called gum spirits of turpentine, a distillation of the resin from certain pine trees. The product of each species of pine tree has different properties, each of which suited different works.[4] The drying of traditional paint was mostly a result of evaporation of water and could take years. Hardening came generally from atmospheric reaction; the oil binder hardened by oxidisation. This all took time and was retarded by a cold or damp atmosphere. The initial hardening and drying process in oil paints could be speeded up by the incorporation of pigments containing oxygen, and certain acetates and sulphates, but these could only reduce the life of the paints in the long-term. Today's 'liquid dryers' were practically unknown to tradition.

The lifespan of an oil paint depended on that of the binders and thinners, the comparative elasticity of the pigment/binder compound, and the paints' integral porosity. A judiciously formulated paint system was expected to be durable and last at least a generation, but it was recognised that none lasts indefinitely; eventually the binder in an oil paint becomes completely oxidised and breaks up. Finish and undercoats of paint lost by weathering and wear could be restored in two coats without renewing the whole system. Before then, in towns and other places where paint was exposed to hydrogen sulphide and soot, it discoloured and became dull in comparison to its original appearance, so it was quite usual for landlords to require their tenants to repaint their properties every seven years, at least.

Traditional paint was usually mixed on the painter's slab measuring approximately 600mm x 600mm. A small amount of oil and some dry pigment were integrated on the slab by grinding with a half-boulder held between the hands, in a circular motion with hand pressure. In this way the painter could see the whole oil paint laid out in front of him in paste form. Thinning came later. A thin sheet of lantern horn was used to scrape the paint from the slab and into a storage container such as a pig's bladder, though wooden tubs were used for larger quantities. This laborious process was repeated until the required amount was made. When it came to use, the mixture had to be judiciously thinned with oil and turps, and then sieved. In general, the paint was run first through a woven cane sieve and then through one of horsehair. The eventual particle size of the largest pigment fragment in a traditional paint was frequently ten times larger than a modern equivalent, though the variety of shapes and sizes could make quite a dense, but still porous, paint. Water permeability depended on the hydrophilicity of the pigment and its ratio to oil. In a white-lead paint the latter could be as little as 20%, providing a water-permeable film, due to the hydrophilic nature of the white lead and the miscibility of the lead soaps thus formed.

'Historic colour' was not just a matter of tint. Of course there was always a tradition of matching colour to natural things to make a likeness of 'plum', 'pea green', and so on. But certain colours could only be obtained by using particular chemicals. Vermilion, for example, is a sulphide of mercury. Such pigments were difficult and therefore costly to obtain, either by nature or by synthesis. They were much more expensive than the earth colours. While this established a visual hierarchy based on wealth or social superiority, colours were also associated with sensations and superstitions. Red was the colour of Mars, wars, great warriors, powerful government and the triumph of good over evil. The Chinese painted their timber with vermilion to ward off the agents of their destructive devils (termites and woodworm), and red was painted around doorways and over thresholds, perhaps to keep the devil at bay. The window bars in public houses were red-leaded, perhaps conversely, to keep the devil in. Otherwise the usual red was ochre, mostly obtained from iron deposits found throughout the world. Venetian Red, now a synthetic colour, was originally a natural earth. Spanish Brown, as it was known, came from Spain and the Balearic Islands. Similar red earths were obtained in Britain, notably from the Forest of Dean and Cumberland. The red paint of more recent Royal Mail boxes and telephone boxes incorporated one of the most useful discoveries and developments of the early nineteenth century: 'scarlet chrome', which was waterproof.

Blue implied serenity and peace and was used in painted portraits to indicate a high-born woman. The most expensive in traditional terms was that used on representations of the Virgin Mary, known as ultramarine. It is made by separating out and softening the purest deep blue parts of the semi-precious stone lapis lazuli, found in Afghanistan. In the Middle Ages this stone cost more to obtain than gold. The cheaper alternative was synthetic azurite (known as 'vice' or 'blue verditer'), but this was not fast to oil and frequently turned green. A more reliable blue was obtained by sprinkling and spreading crushed blue cobalt glass onto a new white-lead paint base, but this too was expensive. Indigo, of course, is a deep violet blue ('indigotin') mostly used by dyers and extracted from three types of plant. This too was imported and expensive, but it was obtained by house painters as dyers' waste and used as a blue pigment, though it usually needed to be precipitated onto a white pigment base. It was not until 1709 that a cheap deep blue was discovered, not by natural accident as with red lead, but by a chance of alchemy while trying to discover an artificial crimson. This revolutionary new pigment, Prussian Blue, remains in commercial use today – though the old way of making it with blood, vitriol and horses' hooves has been replaced by the chemical equivalents of modern industrial chemistry. Cobalt Blue was discovered in the 1780s and the method of making Ultramarine Blue by chemical synthesis was discovered by a Frenchman in 1824; it was made available on a commercial scale two years later. Other blues have since been discovered and each has been immediately fashionable until found to be commonplace.

Yellow was reserved by the Chinese for their emperors. A pure yellow proved impossible to procure in a form not affected by atmosphere. Until 1880, when Chrome Yellow was discovered and commercially developed, the only strong pure yellows had to be varnished to protect them, making them prohibitively expensive. The carriages of the Yellow Earl of Lonsdale were flagrantly costly to paint. In the Middle Ages, gold was simulated in paint by using orpiment, a sulphide of arsenic, but otherwise the most usual yellow was Yellow Ochre, and the brightest and clearest of these are found in the south of France.

The secondary colours were made by mixing two of the primaries (red, blue and yellow) with each other. For example, in combination, blue and yellow produce green. Before the discovery of Prussian Blue, green for oil paint was generally obtained by the use of verdigris (literally 'green of Greece') scraped from corroded copper. Malachite was too intractable and therefore expensive. Green earth ('terre verte') is found in several parts of the world where copper occurs, the brightest being on Cyprus, but it has poor tinting strength and hiding power, though useful on its own. By mixing Prussian Blue with Yellow Ochre, a wide range of greens can be obtained. In 1880 the discovery and development of Chrome Yellow enabled the green equivalent of Post Office red to be made. This was called Brunswick Green, and came in a range of tones from the deep bluish to the lighter yellowish green. Orange involved mixing red and yellow. Pure orange colour was also impossible without unnecessary expense until the discovery of these chromes.

Isaac Newton demonstrated that the appearance of colour results from the reflection or absorption of light rays. The reflection of all the rays of incidental light produces white. Many coloured pigments were enhanced by mixing with an opaque white, which increased the refraction of light. The only pigment used successfully in paint before the 1870s was white lead; all the others became wholly translucent in oil. Known since antiquity, white lead occurs naturally, but was usually made by synthesis – corroding sheet lead with vinegar and carbonating it with carbon dioxide. Vitruvius describes ancient Roman production in jars, using oak chips and vinegar. The Dutch advanced production of white lead to a huge, commercial industrial level, with the development of great stacks in the 1620s, using malt vinegar and horse dung. To obtain white lead and linseed oil for painting, our forebears traded coal, herring, slates, wool and leather at the Staple in the port of Veere, where this trade was conserved for the Scots between 1541 and 1795.

The first sash windows were obtained from Holland in the same way. The earliest sashes were made of oak but still needed putty to hold the glass and stop the joints after shrinkage, and therefore were usually puttied, primed, stopped, filled and painted with chalk-reduced white lead ground in oil. The best finish coat would have been relatively pure white-lead paint, which proved to be superior to other varieties for resistance to knocks and wear and protection from woodworm. Unfortunately, pure materials were very expensive and most of the white lead procured was adulterated with chalk. 'Flake white' described a relatively pure white lead used for finish coats, but Venetian white lead was a 50/50 mix with chalk, and Dutch white lead, mentioned above and commonly obtained for use in Scotland, was only 25% pure. The transparency of chalk in oil made up to five undercoats necessary. (Labour, of course, was relatively cheap.)

Black appears where all the rays of light are absorbed by an object. Traditionally, it was usual to use a black or red oil paint on woodwork. A mixture of soot and boiled linseed oil was easy to procure. Ochre made the oil dry better and was used where it was obtainable and could be afforded, particularly on woodwork and window surrounds of those in the middle sphere of society. A cruder but more durable form of paint coating, for the protection of basic timber from the weather, was hot pine tar cast with sand, also used in primitive earth walls of cottages. The superior equivalent was the casting of stone-coloured lead paint with sand, but even on black tar more elegant lime washes could be overlaid by mixing locally produced lime with a little cow dung.

At first glance the traditional paint system appears to have been little different to that used today. It involved a primer, a base coat and two finish coats, with stopping, knotting and filling in between. The painter required an appropriate primer for each background and this was applied before any knotting, stopping or filling, unlike today. This practice was an economy of effort, since the primed surface showed up the defects. On timber, the pink-lead primer made by adding a little red lead to a thinned, reduced white-lead paint, made better attachment and reduced any suction of oil from the paint and any penetration of damp from the wall. The term 'reduced' became the standard one for any white lead cut with chalk, as most of that from Holland. Bad knots would have been cut out and replaced with matching timber, but smaller knots were dabbed with a mixture of red lead and old oil gold size. On poorer work, where old oil gold size would not be available, animal-skin glue might be used to bind the red lead. On the best interior work, a knot might be covered with silver or even gold leaf.

Next came the stopping and filling. This was carried out in the reduced white-lead paste base which was thinned with a little old oil gold size: this was rather like solid paint and was smoothed thin by knife to leave a good surface. Then came the required number of coats to give either good protection (usually three coats, sometimes five) or the required look (usually two, but sometimes one). Old paint appears very thin and it was applied very sparingly, but it has also eroded to appear thinner, a special characteristic of old lead paints.

Lime washing the ceiling at Craigievar. (NTS)

Almost all traditional paints were applied with a brush. The flat brush generally used today (where brushes are used at all) is a modern invention of the British. The traditional brush was round or oval and the bristles of a new brush were generally 'bridled' with a string 'whipping'. By using it in one direction, an edge could be worn in. New brushes were used for primers and old worn-in ones for finishes. Many painters on the Continent still use round or oval brushes that carry more paint and make the traditionally recommended practice of 'less paint, more painting' easier to achieve. Each paint had its own texture which could be adjusted by the painter, who was trained in this over a seven-year apprenticeship.

Modern paints may be sold as safer, but it is hard for the average person to know otherwise. Some fireproof types, for example, are certainly not. Modern house paints are usually made with price and profit foremost in mind and are clearly quite different to traditional types. They usually require the older coating to be removed for their system to work. Unfortunately this removes much interesting evidence in older houses.

Traditional materials are quite different from today's equivalents. They may have been slower to dry and to use in general, but they were more porous, elastic and durable. Frequently, but not essentially, traditional materials were of local or convenient origin. Paint was the first and last matter of protection to buildings, though it also provided scope for decoration and indication, as in heraldry and signwriting. Colour could be the natural appearance of a paint or an intended tint, which could indicate association or direction, but generally the use of colour followed accepted customs. Today's white is the more blue white of titanium, completely unknown to the house painters of tradition who had to add a little blue to counter the yellow hues of either linseed oil or animal-skin glue. Traditional paints were usually repairable with similar material. We should be better able to identify these materials, their purpose and needs, before mutilating or destroying them.

Some people still paint window joinery white and front doors black without realising the original intention; they certainly do not have durability and conspicuous expenditure in mind when they do. Where black interior joinery is found, it is thought by some that it must be some unknown water-sealant; old red-oxide primers have been mistaken for original colour schemes. It is sometimes thought that all Georgian interiors were in flat oil. In fact they were often oily or contained varnish, and if they were made flat by the use of an excess of turpentine, it was to even out the differential absorption effect of sapwood and heartwood in the background timber; they became flat over time.

The paints of the old tradition were used more economically and artistically and are often inimitable in any other material or binder medium. Traditional paints were made and applied following precepts handed down through generations. They have been tried and developed over centuries, through generations applying common sense and observation. They were generally water pervious, yet also water resistant and certainly reversible. White-lead paints could even be recycled, but if they are surviving well they are safer and more valuable on the wall, rather than being distributed as flakes, contaminating our environment.

We still have a lot to learn about the traditional paint of our forebears. It is easy to be prejudiced against what appears to be their taste but might be the result of more practical considerations, or by apparent evidence of their practice which might really show their sense of taste. In many parts of the world unaffected by European commercial interference, traditional paints remain in use. Our knowledge and experience of the materials and practice of painting tradition depends on realising that our forebears knew what worked from empirical observations over generations; from centuries of handed-down knowledge and precepts of good practice. Since the break with tradition, our knowledge has to be based largely on surviving published literature, but even that dates mostly from the nineteenth century. Since we now care about the nature and the historical integrity of historic Scottish houses, hopefully we will become more aware and appreciative of the painting tradition and traditional paints.

References

The Use of Shingles on Scottish Roofs

1   Bruce Walker, Christopher McGregor and Gregor Stark, *Thatches and Thatching Techniques, Technical Advice Note 4: A Guide to Conserving Scottish Thatching Traditions* (Edinburgh, Historic Scotland 1996).

2   Timothy Holden, with contributions by Bruce Walker, Stephen Carter, Magnar M Dalland and J Andrew McMullen, *The Archaeology of Scottish Thatch* (Edinburgh, Historic Scotland 1998).

3   John Imrie and John G Dunbar, *Accounts of the Masters of Works for Building and Repairing Royal Palaces and Castles* (Edinburgh, HMSO 1982).

4   C F Innocent, *The Development of English Building Construction* (Cambridge 1916).

5   R Hauglid, *Laftekunst: Laftehusets Opprinnelse og Eldste Historie* (Oslo 1980), pp 14, 18.

6   H M Colvin (ed), *Building Accounts of King Henry III* (Oxford 1971), p 34.

7   L F Salzman, *Building in England Down to 1540* (Oxford 1952), pp 228-9.

8   Colvin, *Building Accounts of King Henry III*, p 358.

9   T H Turner and J H Parker, *Domestic Architecture in England* (in three volumes) (London 1851, 1853, 1859), 1853, p 251.

10   Ibid, 1851: 1.335. (Translation: 'The Palace of our Master the King requires a complete covering of shingles'; Dr Steven Green, St Andrews University.)

11   Ibid, 1853: 1.60.

12   C F Innocent, *The Development of English Building Construction* (Shaftesbury, Donhead 1999), p 184.

13   Ibid, p 184.

14   Ibid, p 185.

15   Ibid, p 184.

16   Ibid, p 185.

17   John Alexander Smith, 'Notice of the Shingled Roof of the Tower of the Cannongate Tolbooth, Edinburgh' in *Proceedings of the Society of Antiquaries of Scotland*, sessions 1870-71–1871-72, volume ix, part 1 (Edinburgh 1873), pp 162-4.

18   Ibid, pp 162-7.

Timber

1   F W B and Mary Charles, *Conservation of Timber Buildings* (London, Donhead 1995).

2   T C Smout and R A Lambert (eds), *Rothiemurchus, Nature and People on a Highland Estate* (Dalkeith, Scottish Cultural Press 1999).

3   *Penetrating Damp, Study and Tour, Synopsis of Papers*, SPABiS (Edinburgh 1995).

4   *Toxic Treatments*, The London Hazards Centre (1989).

5   SPAB Information Sheet 14, *Is Timber Treatment Always Necessary?* (Philip Hughes).

6   *Fire Protection Measures in Scottish Historic Buildings*, Historic Scotland (TAN 11, 1997).

7   Note 19; SPAB Technical Pamphlet 12, *The Repair of Timber Frames and Roofs* (James Boutwood 1991).

8   David Yeomans, *The Trussed Roof, its History and Development* (Aldershot, Scholar Press 1992).

9   Timber plus, normally approximately 30mm x 30mm x 75mm long.

10   SPAB Technical Pamphlet 2, *Strengthening Timber Floors* (John E M Macgregor 1973).

11   SPAB Technical Pamphlet 15, *The Care and Repair of Old Floors* (Adels Wright).

12   *Timber Panelled Doors and Fire*, English Heritage Guidance Note (1997).

13   M R Apted, *Painted Ceilings of Scotland* (1966), p xiii.

14   Robert Riddell, *The Stairbuilder and Handrailer* (1860).

Traditional Paint

1   White lead was famously produced in Venice and Rhodes, but the Dutch developed the process to a commercial scale with giant stacks at Amsterdam and Rotterdam in the 1620s.

2   The first was the Scotsman J B Orr, of Charlton, London.

3   White lead is hydrophylic and absorbent of atmospheric gases. Hydrogen sulphide turns surface white lead black, giving paint made with it a grey tone. The trade brochure of Dodd & Oulton, agents for J B Orr & Co Ltd of Charlton, London, manufacturers of Duresco washable distemper, includes advertisements for Orr's Charlton White oil paint and a letter of commendation referring to the painting of Dundee East Station, where a paint trial remained white and repeatedly washable.

4   Venice Turpentine, made from Tyrolean larch balsam, for example, provides the flattest film and is essential in 'japanning' work.

responded eagerly to the opportunity of contributing some observations on the theme of *Caring for the Scottish Home*. The tenth anniversary conference – I had taken part in three previous conferences – seemed to me an important event, symbolising the National Trust for Scotland's effectiveness in bringing together its own highly committed and talented staff with professional consultants in many fields (as well as members of council and committees, the owners of some private houses, and representatives of organisations such as Historic Scotland, the Royal Commission on the Ancient and Historical Monuments of Scotland, the Architectural Heritage Society of Scotland, and others). The kaleidoscope of speakers and participants suggested my own theme: the importance of collaboration in conservation; and of different organisations keeping their own identity and special range of gifts and opportunities, yet working together.

I remember vividly that on my first visit to Edinburgh in April 1976, Marcus Binney and I stayed for a few days with Alastair and Anne-Martha Rowan. Towards the beginning of our visit, Oliver Barratt of the Cockburn Association gave a party, so that we could meet colleagues in Scotland working with historic buildings and landscapes. During the course of the evening, someone turned to me and said, 'Just about everyone who is of any consequence in connection with the conservation of the Scottish heritage is in this room this evening'. This was probably something of an exaggeration, but it impressed upon me two things: one is the fact that the scale of Scotland is an invaluable gift, inasmuch as everyone who works in the heritage field in Scotland can hope to know almost everyone else, or to know enough about them to know when and how it will be advisable to involve them in a particular debate or decision; and the other is the vital importance of being able to meet together at least once a year, and to exchange ideas and problems in a happy, open and positive atmosphere. The role of the annual conference of the National Trust for Scotland is clearly important in that respect, and I would like to see its role expanded so that it is clearly addressed to all those who have the responsibility of caring for the historic environment of Scotland, including its great private houses, park landscapes, gardens and incomparable collections.

When I think of the National Trust for Scotland I am thinking, among other things, of the heroic stories of repairing and conserving Culzean Castle, the House of Dun, Haddo House, Mar Lodge (with its eloquent and indispensable vernacular buildings as well as its wild but managed landscape), and most recently Newhailes, together with their collections. When I think of the great houses and estates still in private hands, I think of the exceptional beauty and tranquility of Traquair House; of the work of William Adam and James Enzer at Arniston and the recent skilful re-creation of the saloon; of the sumptuous baroque state apartment that – remarkably – still survives at Drumlanrig Castle; of the splendours of grand tourism at Hopetoun House and the high standard of conservation there; of the incredible importance to Scottish culture of Abbotsford; of the great kitchen garden as well as the opulent interiors of Manderston in the Borders; and, amongst later houses, I think of the completeness of Robert Lorimer's Ardkinglas in its fine

An Adamesque candle sconce in gilded lead at Paxton House, Berwickshire. An *ad hoc* charitable trust established by the family and the National Heritage Memorial Fund has enabled there to be a long-term vision for the future, with exemplary treatment of the interiors including the rare assemblage of documented furniture supplied to the house in 1774 by Thomas Chippendale.
(PETER BURMAN)

Conservation is Working Together
Peter Burman, *Director, Centre for Conservation, Department of Archaeology, University of York*

Arniston House, Midlothian.
The re-creation of the interior of the saloon is a
triumphant combination of scholarship and craftsmanship, and the determination of a private owner
to see that the right thing is done.
(RCAHMS)

setting. Then there have been the outstandingly successful stories of collaboration and experiment, for instance between Historic Scotland and the National Galleries of Scotland, in the repair, conservation and presentation of Duff House, and the mixture of private and charitable and public generosity – not to mention scholarship – which has been brought together at Paxton House, together with its important educational mission. Scotland is indeed a remarkable country.

I have seen this spirit of collaboration elsewhere, most recently at Schloss Wartin in Pomerania in the State of Brandenburg, where in the wake of *die Wende* – the complete turnabout in affairs following the fall of the Berlin Wall and the reunification of the two Germanies – Professor Joachim Mengel and Dr Charles Elworthy have rescued and repaired a multi-layered country house of the late seventeenth century onwards. This house serves not only as their weekend home – they are both busy academics in Berlin during the week – but as a centre of community and hospitality, as a focus for music and drama, and as the seat of the 'European Academy in Schloss Wartin', an initiative that brings together scholars and practitioners in many fields for the development of debate and new insights in a spirit of friendship and openness. Country houses in tranquil surroundings are ideal places for the development of such initiatives and, run wisely and imaginatively, they can involve very many people without spoiling the very special atmosphere. I will not easily forget a performance in 2000 by a young troupe from Berlin of the play 'Art'. It drew upon the special atmosphere of the house and garden to present a drama in which the friendship of three young men was jeopardised by the purchase by one of them, for a very large sum of money, of a picture that seemed to be nothing but a piece of canvas painted plain white. Was this a case of the emperor's new clothes? Was it a reminder of the fragility of human relationships, and of our capacity to manipulate one another? The play raised delicate and disturbing questions, but what was also remarkable was the quality of the debate that was stirred up by the play in a castle and garden in a remote (some would think) corner of Europe. The play has been performed to critical acclaim in Paris, London, and Berlin; and now, one might say, in Wartin.

I deduce from this that the houses and gardens of the National Trust for Scotland and of private owners in Scotland (and by extension in England, Wales, Germany, France, Italy and all other countries where this phenomenon is known) have incredible opportunities in this new century of ours. We have a curatorial duty towards them – they can be and should be well maintained, with all the knowledge and professional skills at our command. We have a duty of scholarship to understand them, their history and cultural value; and this understanding embraces also their gardens, their park landscapes, and their wider social and economic contexts.

At Harewood House near Leeds, this is being accomplished by a series of scholarly exhibitions of which one, on 'The Art of Thomas Chippendale, Master Furniture Maker', was quite exceptional in its presentation and scope. It had not only a superb catalogue but also a video on the restoration of the state bed, one of the most sumptuous pieces of furniture made in Britain during the eighteenth century. The exhibition programme, and much of the admirable conservation work and study of the house in its setting and its collections, is facilitated by the establishment some years ago of the Harewood House Trust. But this exhibition was also an example of collaboration between Harewood and the owners of other private houses, and with the Yorkshire Region of the National Trust. Such great houses have the opportunity to bring people together in a special way and to be theatres of experiment, inventiveness and community.

I must also emphasise the value of learning from other, sometimes unexpected, sources. In Britain we can learn much that is valuable about houses (preserved and often still lived in and open to the public) from the way in which churches and cathedrals are looked after, and how they are used for a combination

Tōshōdai-ji in the Prefecture of Nara, Japan. A glimpse of the interior of the Golden Hall of the monastery of Tōshōdai-ji. The ancient carved woodwork, including the image of the Buddha, is richly gilded, as is common with sacred images and interiors in many cultures.
(PETER BURMAN)

Conservation is Working Together

of sacred and secular purposes – including being open and welcoming to the public – and the way in which they present and even market themselves. I have also been in Japan, where I found a number of valuable insights as a result of visiting some of the major temples – World Heritage Sites in and around Nara and Kyoto. At one in particular, Tōshōdai-ji in the Prefecture of Nara, I had a long talk with the architect, Mr Yoshio Imanishi, who maintains a site office and works closely not only with the National Commission for Heritage in Tokyo and the local officials of the Prefecture of the Nara, but also with the Abbot of the monastery. (I was delighted to find that all the great monasteries I visited were living communities of monks with a continuity of ritual that went back, in many cases, to the eighth century.)

Here they had a particular challenge: how to deal with the structural problems of the Kon-dō (or Golden Hall) which had been repaired and modified in the late seventeenth and late nineteenth centuries. The wisdom as I received it was that, at the drop of a hat, Japanese architects and conservators would disassemble and then reassemble their important monuments using all the superb skills of craftsmanship at their disposal, and in doing so they would not scruple to make such changes as seemed to them expedient or appropriate. So it was impressive to come up against the reality, wherein Mr Imanishi and his team have been patiently studying the problems of the structure of the Golden Hall for a number of years, making the kind of careful study (from observations and measurements, and using archive material) that in Germany goes by the name of *Bauforschung* – a profound study of a building using the whole apparatus of scholarship and analysis.

Even now Imanishi is hesitating whether to disassemble the structure or not, though the weight of informed opinion seems to be in that direction. He will take the step only with extreme reluctance and after the closest further consultation with his local and national colleagues. This seems to be an admirable attitude to a complex problem. I also discovered that he had on site all the drawings that were made for the late nineteenth-century restoration. This willingness to be thoroughly informed about the interventions of the past is not something I have met everywhere, in Britain for example. Yet another admirable practice, which we could do well to emulate here, is the fact that in Japan the reports made at the conclusion of signif-icant conservation projects are published and copies are not only circulated to key professionals (as we could easily do in Britain, if we had a mind to), but also to the principal regional libraries. In so doing, any member of the public, researcher or conservation professional has the chance to consult them. Since this practice has been adopted, about 2000 reports have been published and disseminated in this way.

This brings me to a practice that is now developing in Britain as well as in certain other countries, and where the National Trust for Scotland has even taken the lead: the preparation of conservation proposals according to recognised international norms (particularly as developed, in a very practical way, through the Burra Charter – the Australian development of the Venice Charter). These not only stress the vital importance of identifying Cultural Significance, but also suggest a way of arriving at this identification. This way of coming to an understanding of the peculiar qualities and values of a particular building or place has been focused for us in Britain by the process of researching and writing a conservation plan.

What is a conservation plan? The most succinct answer has been given by Dr James Semple Kerr, the doyen of conservation plan consultants in Australia: 'A document which sets out what is significant in a place and, consequently, what policies are appropriate to enable that significance to be retained in its future use and development.'[1]

I was personally engaged in the research and writing of a conservation plan during the year 2000 for the Cathedral and Abbey Church of St Alban. The process has been a fascinating and absorbing one (and I hope useful to the community to whom that particular conservation plan is addressed). Among the reasons why participating in this process is so rewarding and enriching is the fact that the consultant has to engage with the community which uses the building or place, as well as with the place itself. In this context I bear constantly in mind some wise words uttered by Dr Richard Gem at the conference 'Conservation Plans in Action' organised by English Heritage at St John's College, Oxford, in March 1998:

> *It is my view that the achievement of a comprehensive and authoritative*
> *Conservation Plan for a cathedral should be a process taking perhaps*
> *several years of work. What would be achievable in the short term might be*
> *an outline Conservation Plan identifying the various areas of heritage*
> *significance, summarising what is reliably known on current evidence, and*
> *pointing to areas of necessary further research.*[2]

What is true of cathedrals in England is surely also true of major country houses in Scotland, or indeed of historic properties of any scale anywhere. A valuable 'Edinburgh perspective' was given at the same conference by James Simpson of Simpson & Brown, Edinburgh – no stranger to the National Trust for Scotland. He pointed out that we do not practise architecture or conservation by numbers, meaning that the conservation plan process should not be interpreted as an opportunity for a consultant to hand down policies and a plan of action which the architect or other professional has then blindly to carry out. He also pointed out that 'if a building or site is to be genuinely sustainable, economic and environmental criteria must be considered' as well as cultural criteria, and 'all of these in an integrated way'; and that the 'scale and ambition of a Conservation Plan needs to be appropriate … the importance of a building or site may be easily assessed on the basis of a limited number of simple facts. A proper balance must be struck'. There is much wisdom also in his concluding words:

> *What I hope for … is the addition of economic and environmental criteria to*
> *the analysis, and the replacement of the 'Statement of Cultural Significance'*
> *with a 'Statement of Values' and an 'Analysis of Objectives', leading to a*
> *broader, more balanced, and more integrated conservation policy. For as*
> *Architecture is about Commodity and Firmness as well as about Delight,*
> *so is Conservation about Economics and Environment as well as about Culture.*[3]

At St Albans a great deal is known about the abbey, now the cathedral, and its former precinct through documentary and archaeological research, some but not all of which has been published. It is a great delight as well as privilege to sit in the Muniment Room, high up over the south presbytery aisle and reached by squeezing one's way behind the eloquent pillars of the late eleventh-century arcading of the south transept, and to be able to match the handling of original archival material (faculties, letters, bills and other documents of many kinds including engravings, watercolours, old photographs and architectural drawings) with the evidence that presents itself to your own eyes just outside the Muniment Room door. In fact the making of a conservation plan seems such a sensible process that I find myself wondering how it could be that important decisions were often made about changes to important historic buildings on a foundation of very modest knowledge. But there it is – we ought to be making some sort of progress in the field of conservation, and I believe that we are.

Engaging in research and synthesising 'what is reliably known' is one thing, but how about the policies? Here I believe it is important that the conservation plan consultant draws upon the experience and wisdom of others: in a cathedral this includes the Dean and the Canons; the professionals who are engaged in the care of the building and its works of art and surroundings (the cathedral architect and archaeologist, conservators of sculpture, the wall-paintings and painted ceilings, the clerk of works, the head verger and his team); the specialist users such as the master of the music (St Albans has an International Organ Festival as well as the daily round of liturgical services); knowledgeable members of the congregation, guides and welcomers; the cleaners (actually there is only one at St Albans, who has to work extremely hard), plus the unremitting work of the vergers; the ladies who 'do' the flowers (an important contribution in itself to the sense of life, vitality, beauty and presentation of the cathedral); and so on. I was very struck by a remark of James Semple Kerr's:

> *One of the major benefits of the conservation plan process is its potential for the resolution or, at least, reduction of conflict by consultation with, and involvement of, interested parties. The process can be effective at both assessment and policy stages if the parties are listened to attentively and their suggestions either worked into the text or acknowledged by an argument that sets out clearly why one of several alternative solutions may be preferable. It is an informal process by which a competent and experienced practitioner becomes both conciliator and arbitrator.*[4]

This is a wise and helpful insight.

I have also found it extremely helpful to evolve, gradually and patiently, a series of policies in draft that I try out on members of the cathedral community as

Cathedral and Abbey Church of St Alban. The Lady Chapel was much restored externally by Lord Grimthorps and internally by John Oldrid Scott between *circa* 1890 and *circa* 1900. Adding a layer of history in that way becomes part of the cultural significance of the place.
(PETER BURMAN)

we walk together about the building and its wider context. It is important, it seems to me, that the consultant has clear ideas of his (or her) own, but that he does not think he has all the right solutions up his sleeve. So the draft policies are gradually being modified and, I believe, made more responsive to the realities of the situation, including (as James Simpson has so eloquently advocated) their economic and environmental aspects.

A particular challenge at St Albans is to evaluate the contribution of Lord Grimthorpe, the overbearing, wealthy and undoubtedly gifted amateur architect and generous donor who, between the death of Sir George Gilbert Scott in 1878 and the late 1890s, totally transformed the exterior of the eastern arm of the building, the transepts and the west front, and some (though fewer) aspects of the interior. Whatever one may think of the way in which he disposed so cavalierly of the perpendicular west front; or whatever the necessity through stone decay may have been to carry out so total a refacing of the Lady Chapel at the east end of the cathedral; or whatever one may think of his decision to invent completely new and somewhat eccentric window forms for the north and south transepts – there is no denying the fact that Grimthorpe made a profound difference to the cultural significance of the cathedral. But was it a great cultural achievement or a cultural disaster, and should any of it now be reversed? To the second half of the question, I would say not. Although I regret some of the interventions of the 1980s and 90s that swept away major furnishings designed by him and removed the complex geometrical lead-glazing patterns of his vast rose window in the north transept, these changes, too, have become part of the cultural significance of what we now have. At the same time, I could not envisage a conservation plan for a living building such as a cathedral or a country house which takes as its starting point the idea that there should be no further changes and no further layers of history. It is surely more a case that we should neither add nor take away without a proper understanding of what is there already. We may have to work extra hard if what we have already is not personally sympathetic to us.

The Cathedral Architect for the past quarter of a century, Andrew Anderson, has himself made some changes or additions to the building which have now begun to take their place in the continuum of time. These include some delicately-judged furnishings and works of art, such as the cross and candlesticks

Rievaulx Abbey. A view of the monastic ruins, cared for by English Heritage, from the no less important early 18th-century Rievaulx Terrace, cared for by the National Trust, with its temples at either end and the rides cut through the woodland below to frame views of the abbey.
(PETER BURMAN)

Conservation is Working Together

in the Ramrydge Chantry, and the new altar table in the north transept which reuses an immense medieval *mensa (*or altar slab) on a wooden framework; and, most substantial and most memorable, the 'Michael Stair' that leads down into the south transept from the first floor level of the Chapter House, in a manner reminiscent of a medieval monastic night stair and with a conviction and quality of craftsmanship and design which recalls the Arts and Crafts Movement. The Chapter House itself, opened by Her Majesty the Queen in 1984, is one of the largest and most significant late twentieth-century additions to any European cathedral (though there are others, such as the three-storey Treasury at Münster Cathedral in Germany, which have been carried through with equal aplomb).

When I think of 'working together' in my local English context, I realise what wonderful opportunities there are for the different responsible authorities to work together. In North Yorkshire, for example, we have the private estate of Duncombe Park, a great eighteenth and nineteenth-century house open to the public with garden and grounds. Nearby (in fact still on the estate, though in the guardianship of English Heritage) are the matchless ruins of Rievaulx Abbey. Above the abbey ruins, and also formerly part of the estate, is the Rievaulx Terrace. This is an eighteenth-century landscape concept in which the terrace and the temples at either end draw into the experience of being there the abbey ruins and the wider landscape of the whole valley, through a series of rides cut into the woodland. Each property is open to the public and each has worked hard at presenting its respective significance to the visitor, but to understand and enjoy all the nuances and the richness of the total concept, you really need to experience them all. For many visitors this might not be practicable, but at least you could now understand at any one of the three properties how they all relate to one another.

One way in which to work towards a contextual understanding of properties might be to commission interlocking conservation plans for adjoining sites, or for sites whose total significance depends on a nearby site. This enterprising approach has been adopted at Lincoln, where conservation plans are being prepared *pari passu* and in consultation with one another for the cathedral (Dean and Chapter of Lincoln Cathedral), the castle (City of Lincoln), and the magnificent and largely ruinous Old Bishop's Palace (English Heritage). May there be much more of this kind of collaboration throughout the British Isles.

The owners of more modest listed buildings have been in agreement that in principle this would be beneficial. One example is Brodsworth Hall Estate in South Yorkshire, owned by Mr and Mrs Ronald Williams. Brodsworth Hall is now one of the jewels in the crown of English Heritage. Mrs Williams (who is an architect) herself worked on its restoration, and she is now working with her husband to ensure the survival of the several fine listed farmsteads on the estate. The repair of the Gothic eye-catcher known as 'the Belvedere' has recently been carried out with the assistance and encouragement of the local authority and English Heritage, and a determined start has been made on the farm buildings. A conservation plan for all these buildings, or groups of buildings, would enable appropriate and consistent conservation-orientated decisions to be made, again incorporating the economic and environmental aspects, and the important fact that farm buildings have to be useful to survive.

Conservation plans could form part of the 'biography' of a building, the kind of imaginative idea we need if we are to engage a whole community in conserving the historic environment. As in Australia or Japan, conservation plans

The Gothic eye-catcher known as 'the Belvedere' on Brodsworth Hall Estate.
(PETER BURMAN)

could be published to the wider world, or at least be made widely available to members of the conservation community so that awareness of what is happening can be more widely spread. It is astonishing how little is published about the conservation process in Britain, though there have been some honourable recent exceptions, such as the National Trust's publication on what happened after the fire at Uppark, and that of English Heritage on what has been discovered at Windsor Castle as a result of the fire there.[5] My worry is that these are probably known largely to conservation professionals only. However, the National Trust's exhibition at Uppark is probably seen with delight by most visitors to the house who could hardly experience it without a greatly enhanced understanding of the significance of the place and of the processes of decision-taking in the conservation process.

It is sometimes said that the heroic period of the two National Trusts is now to some extent over, that they have just about as much responsibility as they can carry, and that the future will be more one of consolidation than growth. I am not so sure. We live at a time when radical and innovative ideas are being put forward for just about every institution, and that is right, and it is in many ways encouraging. But the ownership and development of exceptionally rich cultural assets requires the long-term view, and that is something that the National Trust for Scotland and (in England, Wales and Northern Ireland) the National Trust are well equipped to take. Moreover, it is a vision that needs extending if our vulnerable historic and cultural environment – which includes wild and agricultural landscapes, designed landscapes and gardens, vernacular buildings, as well as great houses and churches, and collections of all kinds – is to survive without further and ruinous incursions. I would argue that the role of the two National Trusts needs to grow and develop, and that two important strands in this development should be a strong commitment to scholarship (and a deepening of understanding of the cultural resources which lie in their hands); and an increasing commitment to working with local authorities (the developing regional authorities and bodies such as Historic Scotland, Cadw Welsh Historic Monuments and English Heritage, and private owners of important aspects of the heritage). Those responsible for churches, cathedrals and other sacred buildings and environments, ought also to be included. Conservation is infinitely more effective when we are working together, and are seen to be doing so.

References

1   James Semple Kerr, *The Conservation Plan: a Guide to the Preparation of Conservation Plans for Places of European Cultural Significance* (The National Trust of Australia (NSW), Sydney 1996).

2   Richard Gem, 'Making Conservation Work in an Ecclesiastical Framework' in *Conservation Plans in Action: Proceedings of the Oxford Conference* (English Heritage 1999).

3   James Simpson, 'Conservation Plans – an Edinburgh Perspective' in *Conservation Plans in Action.*

4   James Semple Kerr, 'Opening Address: the Conservation Plan' in *Conservation Plans in Action.*

5   Steven Brindle and Brian Kerr, *Windsor Revealed: new light on the history of the castle* (English Heritage 1997).

Until recently there has been very little interest in Scotland's historic interiors. In 1935, when Francis Bamford was writing a book on Edinburgh with Sacheverell Sitwell, he recalled:

> I first became curious as to the identities of the men who supplied the furnishings for the New Town of Edinburgh when that splendid exercise in urban planning was first built. But though I made many enquiries in the city's museums and antique shops, and of such of Edinburgh's cognoscenti as were then known to me, I failed to elicit even one name. Most of those I asked believed the furniture for the New Town must have come from London.

Scotland's own sense of cultural identity enshrined in her museum exhibits focused on a remote past, with its heroine Mary, Queen of Scots. For anyone with a latent interest in the Scottish home, there was little to satisfy that curiosity or inform that passion. Although pioneering journalists like Thomas Hannan had begun to write photographically illustrated articles on Scotland's more famous castles and country houses, no museum attempted to showcase more recent Scottish craftsmanship than the mid sixteenth century, after which national taste had merged with that of England, and nobody had attempted to bring together a set of period rooms reflecting historic Scottish patterns of living, as was commonplace in Scandinavia or Europe.

Although a few homes and birthplaces of famous Scots like Robert Burns, Walter Scott and Thomas Carlyle had long been open to public view, their displays reflected old-fashioned museum practices with relics in cases, rather than attempting to conjure up how these buildings had been lived in as homes. Even after World War II, when a trickle of country houses began to open their doors (like the National Trust for Scotland's houses at Culzean or Hopetoun), the emphasis was purely on visual qualities rather than explanation. (The National Trust for Scotland was one of the first charitable trusts to be established to protect a historic house.) Although a great deal of legislation has subsequently been enacted to protect historic buildings of all types, there has been a perhaps understandable reluctance on the part of Government to protect interiors and interfere with personal liberties.

In the late 1980s, after I had spent ten years collecting material in the National Monuments Record of Scotland, I felt I had brought together enough historic material to attempt a book on *The Scottish Interior*, following an American model. However, the London publisher whom I first approached (as they had produced similar subject matter) dismissed my subject as hopelessly 'provincial'. Edinburgh University Press were more brave, but even they were reluctant to consider colour illustrations, which made my visual sources appear colourless. It is only in the late 1990s that matters began to change, and the new displays in the Museum of Scotland are a decisive and deliberate step forward in reflecting the vitality, originality and diversity of Scotland's interiors.

This spirit is now being fed back into the much wider range of houses

Willie Ingram in his kitchen, Keith, Moray.
(SCOTTISH LIFE ARCHIVE, NMS)

Caring for the Scottish Interior

Editor: Ian Gow

that are open to the public, and even the birthplace museums almost all conventionally reflect a domestic ambience, their old showcases banished. In 1982 the Trust bravely added the Tenement House in Glasgow to its collection of properties and it soon took its place as one of the most popular and most loved by members.

It is perhaps inevitable, given the diversity of Scotland and the Scots, that there should be tensions, at a time of an increasing sense of nationalism, inherent in definitions of Scottishness. There is thus a tendency towards fragmentation in the study of the Scottish Home, where an art historical interest in the development of important designers like Robert Adam or Daniel Cottier is sometimes set in opposition to the almost anthropological interest in the couthie vernacular of the farm labourers' bothy. Fascinatingly, with our recent experience of devolution, the Scots seem to be particularly ill at ease with our one contribution to a national style of European interest – our nineteenth-century experiments in the Scotch Baronial Revival with its elemental interest in rubble and antlers.

But what is not in doubt is the need to stimulate more research in order to promote a greater understanding and refinement of our ideas about what constitutes our national identity. In the first essay of this chapter Annette Carruthers, Lecturer in Museum and Gallery Studies at the University of St Andrews, poses a number of approaches to the Scottish Home and suggests lines for further enquiry. She is especially well equipped to question our current assumptions as a result of her work in the National Museums of Scotland from 1991-94, funded by a Fellowship from the Leverhulme Trust, on 'Form and Function in the Scottish Home, 1600-1950'. It soon became obvious that one person could not hope to grapple with such a broad subject area and she therefore concentrated, through a stimulating series of study days, on bringing together a wide range of specialists working throughout Scotland – few of whom had ever met each other – to share their research with an ever growing and very loyal and enthusiastic audience. These pioneering study days found a more permanent memorial in *The Scottish Home*, published by the National Museums of Scotland, which she edited in 1996.

Wright and Mansfield 'Adam Revival', 1880s, at Haddo House, designed by William Adam in the 1730s.
(NTS)

A Home, not a House:
The Development of the Scottish Home

Annette Carruthers

Many fascinating issues are raised by the study of the 'home' rather than the 'house', adding layers of complexity to an already wide-ranging subject. Matters of form and material, location, historical background, the interaction of architect, builder and client, and perhaps the later adjustment and alteration of buildings, are in the traditional province of the architectural historian. The study of the 'home' starts from where the architectural historian usually stops, and is concerned with the use of the building for living – by people in different periods of time, sometimes over generations, in the same house, and by people of different age groups and interests and social groupings.

Methods of research come from social history and anthropology as well as from architectural and art history. Under the general heading of material culture studies, these methods involve sampling across the range of goods used in a particular culture, as well as the detailed study of designed objects by identified architects, artists or makers. It is nevertheless impossible to cover the whole field, because whereas 'house' can be one of a series of virtually identical dwellings, for example in the New Town of Edinburgh or a 1920s council housing estate, every 'home' is different. Within the basic shell the furniture and fittings are brought together by the inhabitants in a unique combination. There are discernible patterns, however; some universal, some common to domestic life in much of Europe and the Western world, and some specific to Scotland because of particularities of the land, climate, materials, economics, politics and law. It is these patterns that we look to identify in studying the home in Scotland.

Because the idea of 'home' is emotional rather than rational, it is necessary to be vigilant for assumptions about meaning. Present-day ideas about the home have developed essentially from nineteenth-century attitudes engendered by the effects of the Industrial Revolution, reinforced by world wars, and entrenched more recently by images in the mass media. Deeply held assumptions, about, for instance, gender roles or cleanliness or the availability of power for heating, can lead to mis-interpretations of the past. Some aspects of domestic history, such as the smell of a town house over a ground-floor byre or the daily experience of a damp miner's cottage with shared midden, can probably never be recaptured, though imagination may provide some insight into past conditions.

There is an additional danger that those who have received training in art or design history, which includes many curators, have been inculcated with ideas about the value of the work of designers and makers of the past and about the importance of the old in relation to the new, which are not shared by everyone. The Romantic idea of the artist as hero-genius has been strongly challenged in recent years but it dies hard, and certain periods of history are also considered to have been more important for the arts than others. These ingrained attitudes have led to a bias towards an interpretation of the intentions of the designer rather than the contri-bution and additions of the occupiers. An inclination in this direction is reinforced by the fact that studying the individual artist is often easier than researching the diverse sources needed to understand the artefact – the home.

Given these cautions about the sheer size of the story to be tackled and the leap of sympathy required to comprehend some of the issues involved, some important factors in the development of the home in Scotland may be identified.

One vital influence was mobility and different patterns of mobility in different sections of the population. Seasonal moving was much more common than it is today. Members of the aristocracy and gentry travelled from their country houses and villas to the capital, whether Edinburgh or London, for the social season. Working people moved often for their work, both in country and in town, and although people of the 'middle ranks' were likely to be more settled because they were running businesses, many in the nineteenth century took their families to the country or the islands to get away from unhealthy city air. Until recently Scotland has had a majority of people renting their homes, and the annual flit to better or cheaper accommodation, as dictated by circumstances, was quite common until well into the last century, as described for instance by Catherine Carswell in her Glasgow-based novel, *Open the Door!*

Houbie cottage interior, Fetlar, 1963.
(SCOTTISH LIFE ARCHIVE, NMS)

A gradual move away from dependence on nature is related to these seasonal aspects of domestic life, and has occurred because of the development of technology for fuel, lighting and labour saving. Connected in turn to this is urbanisation, the movement of the population from the country to city which started in the eighteenth century and increased in the nineteenth, so that by the Census of 1891 the majority of the Scottish people lived in urban areas. Other developments occurred as part of this urbanisation process, such as the availability of new forms of transport and faster communication networks, and these had an important effect on consumerism, the development of goods and the growth of a cash economy. A major change, from a user to a consumer culture, took place in Scotland as elsewhere, gradually encompassing most of the people.

Another very important aspect was the development of privacy for the individual within the home. Changes in attitude were inevitable as people experienced living in houses with more than one or two multi-purpose rooms. This is another area where a leap of the imagination is required to try to understand how material circumstances affected everyday life and feelings in the past, and it is too complex to go into here, but it is no coincidence that Virginia Woolf's great feminist tract is entitled *A Room of One's Own*. There is also an experience gap here between those who prefer privacy and those who like company, and our interpretation of the past will depend on which side we take.

The 1996 book on *The Scottish Home*[1] treated the home as a series of developments from multi-purpose rooms used for general living, to rooms with specific names and specialist uses within a larger structure. Thus the domestic conditions of the majority of the Scottish people were discussed before the houses of the wealthy minority, and the gradual development of the home unfolded in a series of overlapping chapters. The main purpose of this approach was to get away from the idea that style, and a supposed 'trickle-down' of ideas about design, was the most important aspect of the subject – and to try to integrate observations about design with discussion of economic and other vital factors of life.

It is possible, however, to look at it from other angles, and in this chapter I wish to look briefly at the development of the home in different sectors of society, which can be broadly categorised as upper, middle and working class. This is clearly

Canonmills family gathering, Edinburgh.
(THE PEOPLE'S STORY, EDINBURGH CITY MUSEUMS)

a simplistic division and the story is complicated especially by the variation in the landscape of Scotland, but some broad observations can usefully be made. I will conclude with a brief consideration of some of the issues involved in preserving the 'home' rather than the house and, indeed, whether such a thing is possible.

The houses of the aristocracy and gentry show the greatest change at the earliest dates because much of the development of the home is dependent on money, so it is appropriate to start here. It is a well-documented area, not only in terms of architectural history but also in literature and historical accounts, so the story of the development of castles and palaces and their transformation into country mansions and town houses is a familiar one, though always subject to reinterpretation. In brief, this can be seen as the move from the castle to the symmetrical classical house of the late seventeenth and the eighteenth centuries, to the rambling Victorian and Edwardian house, and then largely to a standstill.

Inside, the castle usually comprised a kitchen and offices, a large hall used by the whole household, and smaller rooms to which the family could withdraw. The classical house initially contained a parade of rooms opening into each other and becoming more personal to the owner as the visitor progressed through the sequence. Later in the eighteenth century the arrangement loosened and became less linear. Larger houses with more extensive domestic offices were built in the nineteenth century, both reflecting and confirming changed relations between family and servants. A period of luxury and opulence was followed by decline, and frequently by demolition in the twentieth century, when few great houses were built.

Although these patterns can best be seen in newly designed houses of each period, they were also often imposed on existing buildings which were remodelled to accommodate more rooms or a different arrangement of spaces. Thus, at houses such as Traquair in Peeblesshire or Fyvie in Aberdeenshire, the whole sequence from castle to extensive Victorian country house can be read in the evidence of the structure and the furnishings.

Some aspects of the aristocratic home, such as the possession of comfortable furniture and the development of useful technology, were emulated by people of the aspiring middle ranks. Some were not appropriate to their lives and were therefore not adopted. The parade rooms of the grandest houses, for instance, suited court

Ardtornish House, Morvern District, 1927.
(SCOTTISH LIFE ARCHIVE, NMS)

Caring for the Scottish Interior

Ballachulish domestic scene, 1930s.
(SCOTTISH LIFE ARCHIVE, NMS)

ritual but were not useful for professional or business people. Some developments, such as the expansion in the number of separate rooms, occurred in all strata of society but at different dates, largely because of the financial implications.

Many homes in this group have survived because the straitened finances of the owners in the twentieth century ensured there was not enough money to make changes, though many have been destroyed for the same reason. This destruction, combined with the social influence of many of the owners, has caused the rise of bodies such as the National Trust and the National Trust for Scotland, so we have proportionately more complete upper-class and gentry homes surviving than from other groups. This is also because these houses had rich and attractive furnishings which were expensive at the time and valuable later; they were more durable than cheaper things and were looked after carefully by servants. Large houses can be more difficult to re-use or alter than smaller ones and they are often in remote places in Scotland which are no longer supported by sea transport or by the way of life which sustained them in the nineteenth and early twentieth centuries.

The survival of these houses and the public showing of them has perhaps distorted our idea of what the Scottish home was like in the past, because we cannot experience the middle-class or working-class home in quite the same direct way. An understanding of what some of these houses were like as homes when first built is also affected by the overlying layers of alteration and accumulation. However, they can often be reconstructed in the imagination since the raw materials do still exist and additional evidence from archives, novels, paintings and other sources can be brought to bear. Documentary evidence of houses of the middle ranks is also available, though the houses themselves are often altered beyond recognition.

For the period before the seventeenth century, evidence of the housing conditions of merchants, traders, lawyers, ministers and other professionals in Scotland is sparse. In the ancient burghs such as Edinburgh, Perth, Stirling and St Andrews there is information from archaeological excavations, and from maps and documents, but it is very fragmentary, and although the structures of houses often survive, the fittings and furnishings have been scattered.

Some broad developments can be seen, however. Until the second half of the eighteenth century it was usual for people in the middle ranks of society to have their homes and workplaces in the same premises. This remained common all over the country, but as the number of people in the middle ranks expanded towards the end of the eighteenth century new housing developments such as the New Town of Edinburgh and similar schemes elsewhere were built. A process of separation of work and home began, especially in industrial areas where manufacturing methods caused environmental conditions inimical to family life.

In the new houses there were more rooms with specialised functions, such as separate bedrooms and dining rooms, and new forms of furniture and other domestic goods were introduced to make them comfortable and fashionable. This expansion in the range of goods available also occurred because of the mechanisation of parts of industry and the growth of the British Empire. Developments in textile production, for instance, as a result of new machinery and a worldwide market, led to major changes in levels of comfort and decoration in the home.

The separation of home and work led to the rise of the idea of home as a female preserve, which the 'Angel in the House' was to tend as a haven of calm to which the man of business could escape from the corrupting world of commerce.[2] By the mid nineteenth century this middle-class ideal was well established and to an extent had 'trickled up' to aristocratic society. It certainly influenced ideas in the working-class home and has remained a basic issue in the way we feel about what 'home' is.

During the nineteenth century and well into the twentieth, domestic labour was a major source of paid employment for a large number of people, and the architecture and arrangement of the home reflects the fact that accommodation had to be made for the presence of servants. Similarly, the alteration of servants' rooms into utility rooms and bathrooms indicates changes in the ways that people have run their homes in the past 50 or so years, when service was not an attractive employment option and manufacturers tried to fill the gap with 'labour-saving' technology.

Few middle-class homes survive intact. Architect-designed icons, such as Mackintosh's Hill House, were preserved first by committed owners and then by enthusiasts because of their distinctive quality. Occasionally personal conservatism or eccentricity has led to the survival of a complete house and contents, as in the case of Tenement House in Glasgow. Otherwise, the middle-class home is a changing entity in which useless but picturesque features, such as ceiling roses or bell indicators, are often retained unless the house is comprehensively modernised, but redundant 'ugly' elements, such as gaslight fittings and old kitchen cabinets, are removed. This selective removal makes it difficult to visualise the domestic environment of the middle classes of the past, even with the advantage of photographs, since cluttered Victorian interiors may have been very attractive in colour, with a charm that is not transferred to black and white photographs – or they may not.

In the twentieth century as before, the home changed to suit the way that

Walter Geikie (1795-1837),
Kitchen interior with woman knitting.
(NATIONAL GALLERIES OF SCOTLAND)

people live. Less formal layout of rooms, the increased use of the kitchen as a social space, and a tendency for children to have their own rooms – and certainly their own beds – all reflect society's attitudes to what is appropriate. Recent developments in computer technology have encouraged many to base their work in their homes again, demonstrating the cyclical nature of domestic arrangements.

If little evidence survives of the homes of people in the middle ranks before the seventeenth century, even less remains of working people's houses. However, since home life was intimately bound up with work on the land, which changed little until the agricultural improvement movement of the eighteenth century (and in many places did not change at all), much can be inferred from later evidence. In addition, the local availability of materials and local conditions of landscape and climate were the essential factors in the shaping of the house and its furnishings, and practical knowledge of those conditions provides essential information.

Until about 1890 the majority of Scottish people lived in rural areas. Most were agricultural workers or fishing people and their houses developed to suit their ways of living; work took up the major part of their lives and was the vital influence on the home. Early illustrations, such as Thomas Pennant's view inside a weaver's house in Islay from 1772 or Walter Geikie's drawings of the 1830s, show work and domestic activities taking place side by side in the same space.[3] Tenancy of land tended to be short term so there was little incentive to build and improve and some pressure to keep possessions minimal because of frequent moves. J C Loudon in the early nineteenth century comments on the fine clothing and poor surroundings of working people in some parts of the country, the inference being that many felt it was not worthwhile to spend money on their homes.[4]

Houses were built of available materials, requiring much ingenuity in parts of Scotland where wood was scarce, so there were distinct regional variations in the form of the house, though not a great variety in plans, which consisted usually of a warm room and a cold one. Many of the furnishings were designed to cope with the problem of keeping warm in a cold and windy climate and many had more than one function, so that communal benches doubled as sleeping places and chairs often had rails on which damp clothes could be dried. Found materials such as twigs, reeds, shells and bones were used to make a variety of ingenious hanging hooks, quirky seats, brushes, skimmers and other implements, so there were many different forms of object in the home, along with a conformity of colour from the fact that natural materials were predominant until the late nineteenth century. Highlights of colour were provided by textiles and ceramics, the textiles mainly home-made and the ceramics usually brought in from Glasgow, Portobello, or Staffordshire from the mid nineteenth century. Also imported, especially in coastal areas, were wooden wares from the Baltic, both plain and painted.

Fishing people had a domestic culture of their own with a particular liking for decorated ceramics, often purchased by women following the herring fleet and sent back for display on loaded dressers. Items of furniture developed in specifically Scottish forms to suit the buildings in which they were placed or to suit conditions in the room.

The 'homeliness' and comfort of such houses must have varied enormously, depending on family relationships, the environmental conditions, and the efficiency of the householders in maintaining the building and organising domestic work. Many people lived with smoke and stour that appalled outside observers and must have been hard for some to bear. Makeshift as they might have appeared, however,

Interior of a crofter's house, Shetland, 1889.
(SCOTTISH LIFE ARCHIVE, NMS)

many of the houses were well-suited to the land and the way of life of the people, they must have been comparatively warm and dry, and many survived in occupation well into the twentieth century. The blackhouse at Arnol which now belongs to Historic Scotland, for instance, was occupied until the 1960s.

Life in these houses was very much governed by the seasons and the rhythm of the day, and must have been quite different from the present, when technology enables us to have constant light and heat. For farming people especially, 'home' must in many ways have been the land rather than just the house, as Lewis Grassic Gibbon conveys poetically in *Sunset Song*.[5]

Changes to houses in the country and the move to greater conformity started with agricultural improvements in the eighteenth century and the building of model cottages by landowners. This process started in the richest agricultural areas, such as East Lothian and Fife, and spread to places where landowners wanted to encourage new enterprise, as at Grantown-on-Spey. Such houses provided a pattern for others when the coming of the railways in the mid nineteenth century brought materials such as cut timber and corrugated iron economically to the countryside, and the 'standard' Scottish dwelling developed, with its stone gable ends and symmetrically arranged front with a centrally placed door.

North Uist interior, 1970.
(SCOTTISH LIFE ARCHIVE, NMS)

Life inside must have remained much as it was, though the spread of the stove and the chimney fire meant less smoke and there were probably fewer drips from the roof. Growing industrialisation in the nineteenth century brought cheaper goods, often from a long distance, such as the ubiquitous American clock. Much greater variety and colour was provided by cheaper textiles, printed calendars and advertising prints, and biscuit tins. Life was still hard in the country, however, with little cash in the economy, and photographs of the late nineteenth and early twentieth century often show rooms papered with newspaper or furnished in a meagre way.

Industrialisation was also taking working people away from the country. Attracted by jobs in service or in factories, and pushed out by the Clearances or the struggle to make a living, many took their chance in the rapidly growing cities, which by 1890 accommodated over half the population. As houses in the countryside became less crowded than they had been, those in the cities became notorious for their unhealthy and overcrowded conditions.

One of the most distinctive urban types of Scottish home was the tenement, an architectural form found elsewhere in Europe but not in England and Wales. There is some regional variation in the architecture and features of tenements that has not been fully studied as yet, but the main experience of 'home' in purpose-built tenements for working people from the late nineteenth century must have been of crowding into one or two rooms – a 'single end' or a 'room and kitchen'. The rooms themselves were large and well-built in comparison to the one-room flats converted from 'made-down' city houses, but statistics show how often families with several children and lodgers lived in overcrowded rooms. In these circumstances, privacy in the home must have been virtually unknown, disease spread rapidly, and much hard work was involved in keeping domestic life running smoothly, if this was possible at all. The very poorest people lived in lodging houses, sharing even a bed with strangers, but such conditions can hardly be called 'home' since the most basic concept of the term surely implies a safe place to sleep?

Although the seasonal aspects of life on the land had mostly been left behind, home life in the city had its seasonal changes too. When it was warm, children spent much of their time in the streets or the stair and there must have been a great difference in comfort between the summer and the winter, when coal-fired ranges tainted the air.

The plenishings of urban houses are known from some surviving examples and photographs, and from the many documents produced by social campaigners working for improvement. Examples of furniture and fittings are also preserved in museums, especially in the big cities such as Aberdeen, Dundee, Edinburgh, Glasgow and Paisley. They are less varied in form than the country pieces because they were usually made in workshops and factories rather than by individuals. They are often multi-purpose because they were kept in a small space and had to be useful, and the bed in various forms must have been one of the most noticeable features of the Scottish household. Attitudes to health and morality and the perceived danger of encouraging incest in crowded houses were important factors in the move away from such conditions in the twentieth century.

Eventually the social campaigns had results and after the First World War rapid changes and improvements were made to the Scottish home. Council houses relieved some of the problems about the availability of houses and raised expec-

Above: Tenement House, Glasgow, parlour.
(NTS)

Right: Tenement House, Glasgow, kitchen.
(NTS)

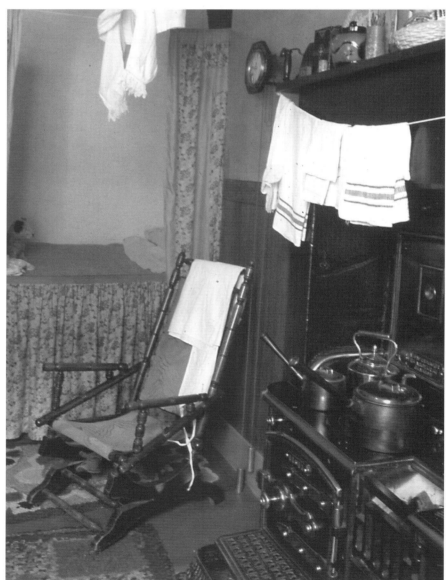

tations of standards, though progress was very slow, and by 1951 over a quarter of the population still lived in houses of only one or two rooms.[6] Major changes also came about through the availability of technology, such as the development of cheaper gas cookers after the First World War, which meant that a range did not have to be kept alight winter and summer for cooking. A small kitchenette then often sufficed instead of the family kitchen, leading to the development of the combined living and dining room.

The homes of working people have rarely survived unless associated with an important figure such as Robert Burns or Hugh Miller, or, like the blackhouse at Arnol, situated in a remote area. In general, the frequent moves of tenants, the late change in Scotland from a user to a consumer society, the goal of improvement, and a legacy of shame about the extreme poverty of the past in some areas, have conspired to ensure that old dwellings and their contents are abandoned and soon disappear.

In Scotland today, 90% of the population lives in urban areas.[7] Contrasts between rich and poor exist as in the past, but the dramatic problems of overcrowding and unhealthy conditions witnessed in the nineteenth century have largely gone. The Scottish home is probably more uniform than hitherto because the mass media provide more information about what people have in their houses to aspire to. Cheap fuel and household goods improve basic comfort, and, as always, changes in ways of living have direct effects on the form and arrangement of the house.

Where conservation is concerned, it is essential to acknowledge that the home, as defined separately from the house, is a constantly changing entity. It evolves with the lives of the inhabitants, altering in response to partnership, birth, success or failure at work, old age, and so on. So the idea of 'the home' is dependent on real life going on within a building, and some aspects of it simply cannot be preserved if it is no longer occupied by the people who have created it. For this reason, those responsible for the preservation of historic domestic buildings and artefacts – family trustees, the National Trusts, museum curators and governing bodies – need to think deeply and develop well-considered policies for this area as a whole, and for each individual building.

Within the framework of protection for listed buildings, those who live in and spend their own money on their houses should be able to do largely what they like with them. Advice needs to be available so that owners can make informed decisions about, for instance, the relative long-term costs of repair or replacement of windows or doors, but otherwise the tyranny of the idea of retaining the original at all costs seems to indicate a lack of artistic nerve. If a privately owned house is open to the public as well as used as a family home, then workable arrangements have to be found to enable it to function, and any alterations might be seen simply as an example of how the home has adapted to present-day conditions, as a parallel perhaps with the addition of Victorian kitchens. If private owners receive public money for repairs, then there should be, and are, agreed conditions about the work to be done and access for the public.

When a 'home' is taken on by an external body such as a National Trust or a national or local government body and is run by curators spending other people's money, there is a duty of care for the historical evidence of the ensemble and the preservation of objects within it which is much greater than that owed by the private owner. The real life and development of the 'home' stops, and the house becomes something else – a resource for information about the past and a visitor experience. It is vital that policies are developed to ensure that both aspects are covered and that the historical evidence does not suffer at the expense of the perceived needs of the visitor. This is not to suggest that no changes should be made in order to present the house attractively, but due importance should be given to the full recording of contents when received, including items such as fan heaters and 'teasmades' that are unglamorous now but may be of more interest in 50 years' time. If this involves educating the public about the importance of documentation and conservation, then this must be made a priority. In addition, it is essential that the role of the curator in these circumstances should be carefully defined.

The house can perhaps usefully be seen as one vast artefact, in which the relation of all the parts to the whole, as well as of the whole to its environment, are important. Scholarship has reached the stage that the general qualities of domestic design are well covered in the literature and what is needed now is more specific information about, for instance, the taste of Aberdeenshire householders in comparison to those from elsewhere. There is much work still to be done on all aspects of the home in Scotland, and it will be rewarding for those who take up the challenge.

Each house must also be seen as an individual, taking into account the length of time it has been occupied, the date of any alterations, and the rest of its history. Houses preserved without their contents should be considered more for their potential as museums or exhibition centres than as recreations of homes, though, like museums, they can also have an important role for the study of the decorative arts and design, of makers and designers. Museum curators, in turn, would be well-advised not to try to recreate the personal nature of the 'home' unless, as for instance at Lauriston Castle in Edinburgh, most of the 'home' survives intact.

At a time when financial resources are diminishing but policies are being explored as part of the new cultural heritage strategy for Scotland, the issue of the preservation of homes of a representative range of people also needs to be tackled. The big houses are disproportionately preserved in the national collection and more consideration is needed of the smaller ones. If it is accepted that the 'home' is an artefact of value for the evidence it provides of the everyday life of the past, as distinct from what the house tells us of architecture and style, then more work is needed to identify and record the full diversity and richness of the Scottish home.

Sanna Bheag, Ardnamurchan, 1930s.
(SCOTTISH LIFE ARCHIVE, NMS)

References

1   A Carruthers (ed), *The Scottish Home* (NMS Publishing, Edinburgh).

2   Coventry Patmore, *The Angel in the House* (1854–63).

3   T Pennant, *A Tour in Scotland, and Voyage to the Hebrides*; *MDCCLXXII*, 1 (Chester 1774), p 229; Walter Geikie drawings are in the collections of the National Galleries of Scotland.

4   J C Loudon, *An Encyclopaedia of Agriculture* .... (second edition) (London 1831), p 1191. This refers to cottagers in Kincardineshire or Mearns.

5   Lewis Grassic Gibbon, *Sunset Song* (original edition) (Jarrolds, London 1932).

6   1951 Census.

7   1991 Census.

As Annette Carruthers reminds us, there has been a very unequal emphasis in Scottish preservation circles on castles and grand country houses with valuable and important contents. But even in these great houses our experience of what it was like in the past cannot but be influenced by the differential preservation of the multifarious kinds of historic materials. Although Scotland was once famed for her home-manufactured textiles, including damasks, carpets and printed cottons, very little has survived the destructive forces of wear, tear and light. For a sense of the importance that textiles once played in Scottish houses, we must look to museums where rare and precious survivals are given the necessary preservation conditions to allow them to defy the effects of time. The most important collection of Scottish textiles, both native and imported, is held by the National Museums of Scotland and is curated by Naomi Tarrant, who is also responsible for the national collection of dress with a dedicated outstation at Shambellie. In her essay Naomi shows the surprising range of materials that once both enlivened and humanised the Scottish interior, which was often less dour than we might think today. Although works of art like the Kinghorne carpet have been enabled to survive allowing us to enjoy its beauty today, it is salutary to be reminded of how much more perished on active service or was recycled as cleaning rags by frugal Scottish housewives.

Sanna Bheag study, 1930s.
(SCOTTISH LIFE ARCHIVE, NMS)

Textiles used in the Scottish Home

Naomi Tarrant

Textiles make a home. They help to provide colour and add warmth, essential elements for converting a house into a home. Textiles are also easily transportable and, in an age when kings and magnates moved frequently from one estate to another to consume rents in kind, this made textiles more important than furniture. The unrolling of large quantities of cloth could transform bare castle walls into an imposing reception hall in moments.

Textiles were not cheap to purchase. They were expensive in terms of basic materials and the labour needed to convert them into fabric, as well as the quantity required for a room. Plain textiles were embellished by being painted or by other more costly and time-consuming means such as embroidery. The development of even more expensive and luxurious woven fabrics, such as tapestries, added to the prestige of textiles, and by the sixteenth century the range for the home was considerable and limited only by the pocket of the owner.

The disadvantage of textiles is their fragility. Furniture, on the other hand, is more robust. Fire, damp, vermin and carelessness can render textiles unusable, either by destruction or disfigurement. Thus, very little in the way of home furnishing textiles survives from anywhere in Europe before 1600, except for tapestries; and for the smaller house, very little before 1700. This inevitably limits our appreciation of their use and importance, and of their original splendour.

The textiles that eventually came to be used in homes can be described as either 'exposed' or 'concealed'. Exposed textiles are those on show, such as window curtains, carpets and wall hangings; while the concealed variety are those used for bedding or cleaning. Plain fabrics survive less well than decorated ones; lengths of

Shambellie House drawing room.
(NMS)

plain velvet or wool wall hangings could always be converted to something else, the best pieces cut out to make cushions or curtains. Similarly, linen sheets served a useful life as rags for all sorts of purposes from bandages to floor cloths, or for making paper. It is also much less easy to date a plain material, whereas those patterned in some way can be dated by the style of decoration.

Textiles that were exposed to general view in a house could be seen in the main reception rooms, such as the drawing and dining rooms, and in halls and stairways. By the sixteenth century, for those who could afford it, wood panelling, at least on part of the walls, was desirable, but above waist level there might be bare plaster walls that could be covered by fabric of some kind.

Of all household textiles, tapestries survive in the greatest numbers. They were used on the walls of the main reception rooms and in smaller closets and bedrooms. Mostly in sets of five or seven, illustrating a story from mythology, history or the Bible, they could also be created as panels with coats of arms or foliage.

Tapestries are woven on a loom. The warps can be of linen, wool or, these days, cotton; whereas wefts are usually of wool with highlights of silk or occasionally metal threads, woven in a densely-packed manner known as 'tapestry weave'. In the fifteenth and sixteenth centuries, tapestries cost more than paintings or other works of art. Nearly all would have been made to order from the original owner, by one of the great tapestry weaving centres in the Low Countries or France.

By the seventeenth century, tapestries were being woven for a much wider market and there was also a thriving second-hand trade. Many of the tapestries found in smaller Scottish homes are known to have come from the Netherlands where agents bought them for clients back in Scotland. By the 1780s, however, tapestries were deemed old-fashioned, and it was not until the late nineteenth century, when the vogue for recreating sixteenth or seventeenth-century rooms arrived, that old tapestries appeared for sale again. The reintroduction of tapestry-making to Britain was started by William Morris at Merton Abbey, and it was from there in 1912 that the Marquis of Bute hired workmen to start the Dovecot Studios in Edinburgh, the only commercial tapestry workshop in Scotland.

Over time, sets of tapestries were broken up, cut down or had holes for doorways cut into them. In the eighteenth century tapestries were often woven with sets of seat furniture to match the panels for the wall, creating a Tapestry Room. Although they are strong, their size, and the weight of wool contained in a tapestry, make them heavy and sometimes awkward to handle. Today the fading of colours and the dirt which has clung to the surface make tapestries rather dull and they are often ignored as just wall covering. However, they repay being conserved. They should be hung using Velcro as this will distribute the weight more evenly, and have a loose lining that will help to protect them from the wall surface.

For those in the sixteenth and seventeenth centuries who could not afford a tapestry there was the possibility of having linen painted to look like one. Very few of these painted cloths survive and none are known from Scotland, but they are mentioned in inventories of the time. Fabric (plain, woven with a pattern or stamped with a design, of wool or sometimes of velvet) could be made into panels to put on walls. These might match the bed if hung in a chamber where there was a curtained bed. Argyle's Lodging in Stirling, for example, has been reconstructed showing the rooms as they might have looked in the late seventeenth century, with matching wall hangings and bed curtains.

There is a large group of embroidered hangings, known as 'crewelwork', that survives from the mid seventeenth to early eighteenth century. These are usually made of fustian, a mixture of linen and cotton, embroidered in coloured wools. The design is the so-called 'Tree of Life', a large trailing tree with exotic leaves, birds and animals. Today it is not easy to work out if these hangings were meant for the bed or wall, although those with a detailed lower border might be considered wall hangings, otherwise their pattern would not be seen. Textile hangings meant for the wall had rings sewn to the back, which would attach onto hooks. This kept them flat against the wall and stopped them flapping when the door was opened, exposing the bare walls behind.

Beds were usually curtained for warmth and privacy, although many for servants or the less wealthy were truckle beds that slid under the main one during the day. Box beds were also to be found. Fully curtained beds might have a fabric top, back, curtains and an inner and outer valance, *ie* panels that hid the rail for the curtains to hang. By the mid eighteenth century, window curtains were more common and so there might well be matching bed curtains. The quantity of fabric needed for one of these beds was considerable. Something as grand as the Melville House bed, now in the Victoria & Albert Museum, would have been made by an upholsterer, but there are records of many women with time on their hands to make them, producing hangings for at least their own beds.

Montgomerie House bedroom, 1948. (RCAHMS)

Stone floors were made warmer by using rushes, but the greater use of floorboards added to the comfort of homes. Carpets were not very common for floor coverings before the mid eighteenth century. Fine Turkish and other Oriental carpets were so costly that they were mostly used on tables. Carpets in the latter style were made in Europe and some were produced in England, including the Kinghorne carpet, a magnificent example with an Indian-inspired design woven with the monogram of the second Earl of Kinghorne and his wife, now in the National Museums of Scotland. Carpets of this quality must always have been rare in Scottish homes, but work or travel to the Orient in the later nineteenth and early twentieth century encouraged owners to bring back examples. Many houses today retain several of these carpets and rugs.

More domestic are the examples of 'Scotch' carpeting, a form of double weave wool where the design is the same on the reverse as the front, except that the colours too are reversed. Made in strips, this form of carpeting could be used in the less grand areas of a house, such as a bedroom, hall and stairs. Because it was reversible, the carpet could be turned when worn and so extend its life. Fragments of these carpets survive in country houses, sometimes as chair covers or underfelt. Another means of extending a carpet's life in areas where there was heavy wear was to use linen or cotton runners. These runners also helped to protect carpets against dirt.

By the end of the nineteenth century there were many different types of carpeting and rugs for use in the home. Machine-made carpeting brought down the price so that more homes could afford it, at least in the main reception rooms. More humble floor coverings included various types of rag rugs, woven with strips of fabric or lengths of wool or fabric hooked in, and often found in nurseries or servants' rooms. More practical was linoleum, with which Kirkcaldy became particularly associated. This was used in bathrooms, kitchens or bedrooms, replacing an earlier type of floor covering – painted cloths.

Curtains for rooms were another element in the early battle against draughts and cold. Wooden shutters helped with this; and for windows without glass there was no point in having curtains. For an important room where guests were to be received, curtains could be elegantly draped at the window and might match any wall or bed hangings. There were various methods of hanging curtains. Bed curtains, for example, were usually hung by rings from a rod. By the eighteenth century pelmets of varying complexity were used in main rooms to hide the way window curtains were hung. Various designs for these pelmets were published in furniture makers' pattern books of the mid to late eighteenth century and they continued to be quite elaborate until the late nineteenth century.

Heavy curtains of velvet or brocade were used in reception rooms, but lighter printed linen and later cotton chintz was used for bedrooms and informal family sitting rooms. These printed fabrics were popular because they could easily be washed. This kept the room looking fresh. Chair covers matching the curtains also helped to make a room look more of a whole, even if the furniture did not match. Chintz was often glazed to help stop the dust penetrating the cotton too quickly, another means of keeping curtains clean.

Upholstered seats on chairs were not common until the eighteenth century, although in the seventeenth some chairs had specially woven covers known as Turkey-work. This fabric had a knotted pile rather like a carpet, but the designs were often rather coarse in execution. A whole set of chairs with Turkey-work covers was ordered for the council chamber in the Palace of Holyroodhouse in 1685 when it was rebuilt. Today surviving examples on their original chairs are rare. More common are the embroidered seat covers that became increasingly popular in the eighteenth century when whole sets were made by women for their homes. One such set is to be found at Blair Castle and many single examples exist in houses throughout Scotland. Grander houses or rooms might have their chairs and settees upholstered in woven silk damask or other fabrics to match the wall coverings, such as those at Hopetoun House. This method of covering seat furniture to match walls continued throughout the nineteenth century; and to this day when restoring these rooms, new fabric replicating the old is often chosen. In the eighteenth century, chair dust covers of checked linen were used to protect delicate fabrics such as silks or embroidered chair covers. These would remain on the chairs when the family was at home and only be removed if guests were expected. An earlier example of protective covers are the green baize 'cases' ordered for the Turkey-work chairs for Holyrood in 1685.

The nineteenth century saw an increase in the types of seat furniture found in drawing rooms and ladies' sitting rooms. New upholstery fabrics were introduced, such as plush, and ways of using these, such as draping or piping, were applied to heavily stuffed seats. More comfortable seating, for example the club chair which was a completely stuffed armchair, required the development of more robust fabrics to cope with its requirements. These new fabrics were often dust traps and could give a rather heavy look to a room. For summer, and again to protect expensive fabrics, loose printed cotton covers were used. These might be removed in grander public rooms for visitors, but in family rooms or more informal environments such as shooting lodges, these covers were permanent. As they were made of washable fabrics, they helped to keep the rooms looking clean and fresh.

Another protective device for upholstered furniture was the antimacassar. In the nineteenth century, men used macassar oil to smooth down their hair and this could rub off and stain fabric-covered seating. White linen or cotton cloths,

Dalkeith carpeting.
(NMS)

usually with matching pieces to go over the arms of an armchair, were introduced. They were often embroidered or trimmed with heavy upholstery lace and were regularly changed. Antimacassars lasted until the 1950s, as the hair cream that replaced the oil also stained fabrics. When men stopped using oils and creams on their hair, chair protection was no longer required.

Other textiles that could be found in rooms included fire and other screens, table runners and mats, footstools and cushions. Large screens were usually made of more robust materials than embroidered fabrics, but fire screens were often elegant pieces of furniture. Those that were used to screen the face from the heat had smaller leaves on adjustable poles, sometimes decorated with delicate embroidery on satin. Other screens were used to hide an empty fireplace during summer and might have a bolder pattern worked in wool on canvas. In the Victorian period adjustable face screens clamped to the mantelpiece were popular. Fire screens, cushions and footstools were typical of the kind of items women embroidered for the home at that time. They often used the bright colours of Berlin wool, soft untwisted wool threads in an amazing variety of colours worked in cross and petit point stitches on canvas, sometimes enlivened by beads. Patterns for these embroideries could be found in women's magazines or bought in fancy goods shops (like the one run by Mrs Jane Gaugain and her husband in Edinburgh from the 1830-50s). The resulting embroideries are some of the most effective textiles found in the home and still exist in large numbers.

In dining rooms the table was usually left without a covering when it was not being used. In some smaller homes, where the dining table might be used for household tasks such as sewing or homework, a protective cloth like felt or chenille might be put over it. Similar covers might be used on tables in other rooms. Where pot plants were put on tables, pedestals or other pieces of furniture, small mats, sometimes embroidered, were used to protect polished surfaces from scratches and water. By 1900 it was common to have long runners down a dining table, and on sideboards if plants or ornaments were going to be placed on them. Sets of these runners and small matching mats were popular items for women to embroider and many patterns are found in women's magazines until the 1950s. These types of protective and decorative textiles were probably more common in middle-class homes than in the homes of the wealthy. Small mats were also found in bedrooms, where dressing table sets of candlesticks, pin tray and powder bowls in glass or ceramics were set out. Mats not only protected the furniture's surface, they also hid the dust, which was not easy to wipe away during the time when open fires were the only heating source in the home. In cities in particular, the general level of pollution from dust and grime made keeping a house clean an uphill struggle. Masking the problem was one way of dealing with it.

The Scots owned large quantities of table linen, which they were proud of and used in abundance towards the end of the seventeenth century. Inventories mention enormous numbers of cloths and napkins, all made of white linen, often in small geometric patterns called 'diaper'. More elaborate designs were worked in damask where two different weaves create the patterns. Designs varied from floral motifs, family coats of arms, Bible stories, commemorative scenes, and patriotic thistle patterns. By 1700 there is evidence that at least some of this damask was woven in Edinburgh and Hamilton. By the nineteenth century Dunfermline was the main centre for this type of table linen. Starched, these white linen damask tablecloths and napkins added quiet elegance to a dinner table.

Edinburgh drawing room, *circa* 1900.
(SCOTTISH LIFE ARCHIVE, NMS)

Damask table linen.
(NMS)

Textiles not generally seen by visitors were those under the heading of 'bedding'. Bedrooms, however, were used for other purposes until more recent times and in many homes beds were to be found even in the main living rooms. It was considered ungracious not to house relatives and friends when required: hotels could be few and far between in country areas, and those in cities often had very unsavoury reputations.

Until the introduction of the metal spring in the mid nineteenth century, all beds contained several mattresses of varying kinds. The number of mattresses on a bed would reflect the wealth of the owner. Usually there was a large sack-like under-mattress filled with straw, chaff, or other coarse material. Its bag was made of coarse sacking or, preferably, more closely-woven linen harn to stop the material inside from poking through. On top of this were one or more tightly-constructed mattresses with strong ticking covers, although leather was sometimes used. These were stuffed with wool or horsehair, tied in place with thread, and finished with decorative knots on the outside. The introduction of metal springs did away with the need for the lower straw mattress; and the interior sprung mattress is a twentieth-century invention.

Sheets covered the mattress to provide a softer layer to lie on, with another sheet on top as covering. These were made of washable fabrics and linen was the favoured material until the mid to late nineteenth century when cotton sheeting became available. Pillows and bolsters – *ie* sausage-shaped round pillows placed the full width of the bed – were made of strong, closely-woven fabric called 'ticking' and filled with feathers. They too were covered with washable linen or cotton covers. One custom adopted by some households was the use of pillow and sheet 'shams', *ie* ornamental covers of white linen or cotton, sometimes with lace edgings that could be removed at night. These were particularly useful if a person was recovering from illness and could receive visitors: the decorative shams provided an easy way of refreshing the visible part of the bedding.

On top of the sheets various blankets were placed to provide warmth. These were usually made of twill weave wool and often white with borders of dark blue in different check patterns. In Scotland, however, inventories list bed plaids rather than blankets. These were probably multi-purpose items that could be used as an outer wrap in the manner of a plaid, but could be put on the bed at night for extra warmth. Plaids for wearing were usually twice the length a blanket was required to be, but blankets were sold as pairs and are described as such in inventories. These pairs could be cut to form two separate pieces or kept as one long length and folded over. The best quality blankets were probably those associated with the town of Witney in Oxfordshire. Another type were known as 'rose' blankets, where the flower was embroidered in each corner of a plain white blanket. By the end of the nineteenth century, blankets came as single pieces with finished borders made in different sizes to fit standardised beds. They featured stripes of various kinds – scarlet and grey for the army, for example, or brown for charities.

Over all this bedding a decorative cover was placed to hide everything during the day when the room might be used for entertaining guests. The cover could match any other exposed textiles in the room, such as curtains, or they could provide a complete contrast in fabric and style. In Scotland there is evidence of decorative embroidered blankets, patchwork quilts, heavily-embroidered silk covers, white machine-woven Marcella covers, crochet, knitted and white cotton lace covers, and, by the end of the nineteenth century, eiderdowns.

Bedroom textiles could also include a nightdress cover or case, particularly associated with children's rooms and school dormitories. It was probably considered a more middle-class item than something found in grander houses. However, even Prince Albert had a watch pocket pinned to the bed head for keeping his timepiece in at night. These pockets were often made at home, embroidered, and presented as gifts to friends and relations.

Another large group of household textiles is towels. When bathrooms became more generally available, towels were often to be found there, possibly draped over heated rails or pipes. However, hand towels of linen diaper were usually placed in bedrooms for use with the washhand basin provided. Looped Turkish towelling made good bath towels, produced with and without coloured stripes; and there were different types of towels for the kitchen and for use in the stables.

Textiles for cleaning homes have not survived in great quantities, simply by the very nature of their use. Many cleaning jobs were done with old rags because fabric remained expensive until the availability of cheaper machine-made fabrics in the nineteenth century. However, one of the growth areas of the mid to late nineteenth century was the variety of textiles available for each cleaning job. The Army and Navy Stores catalogue for 1907 lists different cloths for glass, tea, pantry, basin and lamps, as well as about ten different types of cloth dusters. Recently some of these old fabrics have been reproduced, such as linen tea towels with red stripes, and linen dishcloths, perhaps as part of the increasing interest of the public in using natural fibres.

Old manuals on cleaning make it quite clear that each job done in the home required a different type of cloth. To assist the maids and the housewife, these were often coloured differently. For example, general dusting was done with a blue and white checked cloth, while really delicate work around ornaments on a mantelpiece, for example, was done with a feather duster. Cloths for cleaning out chamber pots were very carefully distinguished from those used for kitchen jobs. This proliferation of cloths was in part due to a better knowledge of hygiene, but it was also an attempt to combat the relentless grime brought to towns and cities throughout the country by industrialisation.

Today old textiles in a home can be a problem as age and fragility might make it impossible to continue using them. Tapestries have a stronger basis than most other textiles and will repay conserving, but any conservation work should be undertaken after discussion with a qualified textile conservator. All textiles suffer from light, both from fading of colours and degradation of the fibres. Protecting them as much as possible is therefore the best way to extend their life.

Edinburgh washing lines, 1965.
(SCOTTISH LIFE ARCHIVE, NMS)

The fragile historic textiles that we enjoy in museums or country houses today owe their preservation to careful housekeeping practices which protected them from light through vigilant blind lowering and the banishment of moths and other household pests. In her contribution to this chapter Wilma Bouwmeester, the National Trust for Scotland's first Conservator, appointed in 1997, shows how modern conservation techniques have been developed to replace the care lavished not only on textiles but on collections of every material under the Scottish sun by the now-vanished band of domestic servants. A new, more rigorous and scientific approach to conservation favours a holistic view and aims to control the environment in which collections are being preserved. This holistic view cannot but lead to the preservation of the very wide range of objects that have accrued in a single, quintessentially ordinary Scottish home like the National Trust for Scotland's Tenement House – except that possibly and probably there is, alas, now nothing else like this remarkable survival.

Caring for Collections

Wilma Bouwmeester

The National Trust for Scotland looks after a substantial number of historic houses, ranging from the great houses like Culzean Castle and Falkland Palace to humble birthplaces and craftsmen's abodes, such as Thomas Carlyle's Birthplace and the Weavers' Cottage. Many are associated with some well-known person or other; many contain items by the hands of famous artists. But no matter how important or humble the buildings and their associations, the collections held inside them are equally vulnerable to the unstoppable process of deterioration. If a painting by Raeburn seems to have survived the ravages of time in a better state than a humble drawing by a farmer's daughter, it is not because of its inherent importance but because more care has been taken to ensure its preservation. For conservators,

Falkland Palace.
(NTS)

the matter is important, not the significance. And conserving the material can be surprisingly down-to-earth, no matter how unique the item or how famous the maker.

Caring for the contents of a home is not a new issue, as is confirmed by Suzanna Whatman's manual with housekeeping instructions, which dates from 1776. In her manual, Suzanna (wife of the paper maker James Whatman) wrote down instructions for her staff on the various issues of looking after the precious contents of her home. Some 200 years later, this resulted in the very popular, but alas no longer available, *Manual for Housekeeping* by the National Trust for England, Wales and Northern Ireland. It forms the basis of collections care for their property staff, our property staff and for many private owners and collectors who have purchased the book since it was first published. The reason for its popularity lies in the fact that the traditional principles of Mrs Whatman are still valid today. The difference is that modern materials and techniques are now being applied where appropriate to achieve the same aims – preservation of our precious items.

Traditionally, conservation activities concentrated on the repair of individual items following deterioration or accidents at a property. Work would be carried out with the aim of restoring the item to its original state and former glory, and this often involved repair, replacement, cleaning, re-upholstery, dismantling and rebuilding. In recent years, conservation has developed into a highly profes-sional area of work, which is reflected in the many courses at postgraduate level and the development of a professional accreditation scheme for conservators. Conservation no longer refers purely to the repair of an item: it also involves many other activities aimed at documenting, stabilising and preserving objects. Two quotations indicate how practising conservators see their profession today: 'Conservation = all actions aimed at the safeguarding of cultural property for the future, including interpretation' (United Kingdom Institute of Conservation [UKIC] Rules of Practice) and 'Conservation is based on a respect for the existing fabric and should involve the least possible physical intervention' (Article 3, the Burra Charter).

Until recently, the traditional approach to conservation described above could also be found within the Trust. This changed with the appointment of a

Cleaning a wall tapestry at Fyvie Castle. (NTS)

Caring for the Scottish Interior

conservator in the Curatorial Department in July 1997. A different language was introduced, and where items once required 'some tender loving care by a housekeeper to polish items to a shine, because they looked shabby, dull, tired and worn', the conservator speaks of 'ageing, character, evidence of the object's history and life, and requiring full condition assessments to determine both preventive conservation actions and treatment to stabilise their condition'.

In order to ensure improvements, priority was given to the development within the next five years of a common goal, an approach accepted and agreed by all. This was achieved in the development of the Collections Care Policy, a document outlining the Trust's aims and intentions in the care of all its collections. It was accepted by the governing body, the Council, in 1999, three years ahead of time. Areas covered by the policy include: *preventive conservation*, including assessment of the condition of collections, monitoring and control of environmental conditions, the impact of visitors and events and record keeping; *remedial conservation*, conducted by registered conservators where possible and guided by information on the background and significance of the collections; *training in collections care activities* for both paid staff and volunteers; the importance of a *planned approach*, including financial planning; and the development and continuation of *partnerships* with related organisations.

Underlying the policy is the aim to reduce the amount of remedial conservation in favour of improved preventive conservation. It should be recognised that after repair of damage an item is no longer the same, no matter how skilful and invisible the repair. Inevitably there will be some loss of material and therefore of information. This new approach is applied to all our collections, grand or humble. The National Trust have also recognised this and the following is an extract from their *Policy and Procedures Paper on Historic Buildings* (1996): 'It is likely that in future we will be the only resource for the study of certain categories of object which may currently be considered by many people to be of little significance.'

Conservation efforts concentrate on actions of a preventive nature, as these have been shown to be the most cost-effective and most satisfactory in the long term. They also benefit entire collections, and therefore allow for best use of limited resources. The aim is to prevent damage and reduce deterioration. From time to time treatment may become necessary to ensure that items are in a stable condition, or to deal with the occasional accident. However, this is only one small part of the whole range of collections care issues and any treatment work should be followed by appropriate preventive measures to reduce the risk of repeated damage or instability. This includes an assessment of the situation in which the item is displayed and the risks to which it is exposed; acting upon the findings of this assessment in order to improve the conditions and reduce these risks; and ongoing monitoring of both the condition of the object and the surrounding environment.

The single most important aspect of providing an appropriate environment for collections is the building in which they are housed. Apart from being of importance in its own right, the building is the first line of defence; the first barrier against wind, rain, light, extreme temperatures, fluctuations in humidity, insects and pollutants. When in good condition, the building acts as a protective envelope around the collections. It can only function as such if it is in a good state of repair, and regular maintenance is therefore paramount. Leaking roofs, blocked gutters and downpipes, and insufficient drainage or cement harling (especially when in poor condition) can lead to a very damp environment inside a building. This will not only cause rot and mould, but will also create the ideal environment for insects, which will then attack the furniture and textiles. In the same way, shutters that are in good condition and function properly will help keep the damaging effect of light to a minimum. It cannot be stressed enough that the building has a very important role in collections care, and this relies on the cooperation and input of those responsible for maintaining and repairing buildings.

The care of collections can be broken down into five areas: monitoring and control of environmental conditions; display; pest management; regular care; and preparedness for disasters. The key to a stable collection is a stable environment. Humidity, temperature, light, ultraviolet radiation and pollutants all need to be controlled to within acceptable levels. In historic house settings this should ideally take place without compromising conditions for visitors and staff and without installing intrusive plant or equipment (for which there is often no space in small cottages).

The first step in this process is to gain knowledge of the current conditions by monitoring them. This should take place over a full year to cover all seasons. Monitoring takes place with thermohydrographs in the small properties, or with electronic sensors and computer analysis for properties with a larger number of rooms. Readings of light and ultraviolet radiation are taken by hand at regular intervals. These results are used to assess the nature of the environment, and to determine what steps should be taken to improve the situation, if necessary. Once this has taken place, conditions need to be monitored again, to establish whether the improvements have had the desired effect and to ensure that conditions remain within specified levels.

For the control of humidity, the principle of conservation heating is applied. This is based on the fact that in a sound and well-maintained building, humidity and temperature are directly related: when temperature goes up, the humidity comes down and vice versa. Temperature is therefore allowed to fluctuate in favour of a stable humidity, and this is achieved by controlling the heaters with humidistats rather than thermostats. The principle was first developed by the English National Trust and is now applied successfully in many of their properties.

Ultraviolet radiation is eliminated with the use of ultraviolet-absorbing film, either applied directly to the window with an adhesive, or provided in the form of blinds in situations where the age and/or condition of the glass do not allow the adhesive method. Light levels are controlled with calico blinds to stop direct sunlight from entering the room and shutters to eliminate all light outside opening hours.

One of the more challenging problems is to display collections in a way that keeps the risk of accidental or long-term damage to a minimum. The taste and use of the original occupants often dictate the layout of rooms. This is respected as much as possible to allow the visitors a genuine experience. The Trust currently allows visitors full access to the rooms on display. In many cases the number of visitors by far exceeds the number of original occupants, and this may lead to accelerated wear of stairs, carpets and other items. The enjoyment of current generations must be balanced against the enjoyment for future generations, and in some cases this may have to lead to the use of barrier ropes or replica items in order to ensure the preservation of the originals.

The two most common pests that cause damage to objects are the clothes moth (silk, wool) and *Anobium punctatum* or woodworm (furniture, books). It is the larvae of both the moth and the Anobium beetle which causes the damage. The

Fyvie Castle chandelier. (NTS)

ideal preventive method is preventing infestation by eliminating insects from the house. Any newly introduced furniture or textile should be checked first and treated if necessary. Flower arrangements in display rooms can harbour insects, although more often it is birds' nests in the chimneys. Insects can fly in through open doors or windows, or come in on visitors' clothing. The latter however are rare occurrences, infested items or birds' nests being the most common sources. The next best option is to prevent any insects that do enter the building from settling and laying eggs. This is done by creating an environment in which they cannot thrive. Insects cannot control their body temperature, nor can they drink. They take on the temperature of their environment, therefore the cooler the environment the lower their activity. Moisture is absorbed directly from the atmosphere and high humidity is needed for this. Their preferred environment therefore consists of dark, damp and reasonably warm undisturbed places with a source of food. This can be an item of furniture or textile, or it can be dust, dirt or other organic debris. Again, the maintenance of the building is important, as the better maintained it is, the less the risk of dampness, and this significantly reduces the risk of pests developing. The most effective way of preventing pests is to ensure humidity levels below 65% and to keep the place clean and aired. Even if an insect entered the house, these conditions will discourage it from settling and laying eggs.

There are interventive methods of treating infested furniture with *Cuprinol*, a poisonous liquid that is painted onto bare wood in spring, when the beetles come out. It is usually only applied to wood without a surface finish, it penetrates only a few millimetres (although this can be improved by injecting it into exit-holes) and only kills the adult when it eats its way through to get out. It may therefore take repeated applications over two or three years before all the insects in the furniture have been killed. The only way of killing what lives inside the furniture is by enclosing it in a tent ('bubble') with a poisonous gas, or with carbon dioxide, which causes a lack of oxygen (the insect opens wide the 'pores' through which it takes in oxygen and humidity, this causes moisture to evaporate

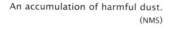

An accumulation of harmful dust.
(NMS)

and the insect desiccates). Apart from all the handling involved in applying these methods, both carry risks of damage to furniture and other items, and the bubble method is quite costly. Both only kill during treatment, and reinfestation is likely unless the environmental conditions are improved. Prevention is therefore definitely the preferred option.

Dusting is not carried out purely for aesthetic purposes, but also because dust can be potentially damaging: it can be acid or alkaline, and combined with moisture this can cause damage. It can be sharp and cause scratching, or it can become embedded in the surface of items. It therefore needs to be removed regularly. This takes place during regular, routine cleaning, usually in the morning before the property opens to the public. But does dusting need to take place every day? Would visitors notice if it were done once every two or even three days? Many of our properties are now so well maintained that much less dust is generated inside and dusting is therefore not needed every day. Less dusting means less touching and handling and thus less risk of accidental damage. By dusting every second or third day the risk could be reduced without compromising the way the property looks. In this way the associated risks can be reduced by 30-50%, a not inconsiderable percentage.

The scent of freshly-waxed furniture is appreciated by many, its main association being with 'cleanliness' and 'good housekeeping'. The application of traditional wax is necessary on furniture in frequent use, to protect the surface and give it a pleasant sheen. However, furniture that is no longer in use, as in our historic houses, does not require protection to the same extent and waxing need only take place once every two or three years. More frequent waxing may lead to a heavy build-up of wax in carved details and may form a sticky layer in which dust can get trapped. Should a waxed item have gone dull, a buffing up is usually sufficient to restore the sheen of the wax layer, which is still present. Traditional wax based on beeswax is the gentlest and the only one suitable for historic furniture. No other waxes or sprays are used on Trust furniture.

Cleaning plasterwork at Fyvie Castle. (NTS)

Disasters do not occur regularly, but when they do the effect can be devastating for entire collections. Three areas need to be dealt with: fire, theft and flooding. All Trust properties, whether large or small, contain fire and burglar alarms, and in some cases individual items are also alarmed with motion detectors. Procedures to be followed are laid down in a Disaster Manual, a copy of which is held at each property with details of local services. Telephone trees to inform head office staff are also in place.

Having outlined the ideal preventive approach to the care of collections, a pragmatic approach is also essential. Assessments of risk need to take place with common sense in mind: there is little to be gained from providing the right conditions for an individual item if a risk affecting the entire collection (such as fire) is not being addressed; there are instances where the handling of items can be a higher risk than the presence of dust. Such a pragmatic approach will help us to get our priorities right. This is what good collections care and preventive conservation provide: an approach that deals first of all with issues affecting entire collections, followed by the improvement of situations for small groups of objects. Within this approach, the most vulnerable groups of items are to be given the highest conservation priority. If the care given to collections is approached this way, it ensures that although damage and deterioration cannot be entirely prevented, the right steps are taken to minimise and slow them down as much as possible, so that generations after us get a chance to enjoy the collections the way we enjoy them today.

Because so few historic Scottish homes survive or are likely to, the written historical record is of particular value. In the concluding section of this chapter, I suggest a few lines of enquiry that might help to stimulate research into particular homes and encourage the process of understanding and recording. Although the future researcher into twentieth-century Scottish homes will have unrivalled opportunities for research in published and photographic sources that are denied to the student of earlier periods, there is no substitute for the first-hand experience of oral history, dependent on the memories of a narrator which are inherently fragile until committed to a written or recorded version. An account of the most ordinary Scottish home, accompanied by photographs and a record of the purchases of its component parts of furniture and carpets, could not but be extraordinary in its rarity and immediacy in years to come. If it happens to be an old house, the changing patterns of use reflected in its adaptation to modern requirements would have an additional fascination, particularly if the changing pattern of housekeeping and the pattern of meals and expectations of comfort were also charted. The most successful historical evocations of particular Scottish houses always seem to have been inspired by the writer having the certainty of a particular audience and readership. The genius displayed by Elizabeth Grant of Rothiemurchus cannot but owe a great deal to the fact that she was writing for her own children in far off Ireland, to give them pride in their descent from a proud line of Scottish Highland chiefs.

Investigating People and Place in the Scottish Home

Ian Gow

I have to say, at the outset, that I have never been very convinced that 'home' is a Scottish concept (as against the more prosaic 'house' where one retreats from the hostile elements), because the Scots have tended to be more realistic than sentimental about their dwelling places. This contrasts to the 'Home Sweet Homery' of our southern neighbours. Traditionally Scots have been satisfied with rented accommodation – given monumental expression in the tenement – and this mobility perhaps contributed to their disproportionate role in the British Empire. Calvinism encouraged unsettling thoughts about the uncertainty of the future even if one happened to be comfortable today. Life in Ivor Cutler's *Scotch Sitting Room* was certainly never cosy.

Because there has been so little study of the homes of ordinary Scots, this is a field in which the amateur can hope to make a real contribution by recording memories and experiences of particular houses. Finding out about one's home must come second in importance only to researching one's ancestors and both these endeavours are the mainspring of Scotland's now thriving local history industry. The interaction of the former owners of a house with local government regulations and state fiscal initiatives cannot but leave a paper trail that can be followed up and unravelled, allowing often intrinsically prosaic facts to be woven into a story.

I have enjoyed 17 years of training in the field of gathering together individually trivial bits of information (at state expense as a result of my work in the National Monuments Record of Scotland) and now I do much the same thing every day with a rather narrower focus on the varied properties of the National Trust for Scotland. But it is quite difficult to set out a format for going about such a task because in my experience so much depends on serendipity and, most importantly, the swapping of information with one's fellow researchers.

Trust properties are relatively easy to research because they usually come with an archive – housed within the castle at Drum – and our colleagues and predecessors have been actively seeking information and writing down interesting facts retailed by our visitors, former family members and domestic staff. We draw on all of these sources in our guidebooks and I do want to stress that a researcher's work is not over until they have arranged the facts and figures in this kind of accessible format for the enjoyment of others. I have spent my life writing guidebooks and am, perhaps understandably, obsessed with them and collect both guidebooks and monographs on individual houses. The latter are surprisingly rare; additions to this genre would be welcome. The most vivid account of any Scottish house must be the childhood memories of The Doune that Elizabeth Grant of Rothiemurchus wrote down for the benefit of her own children far away in Ireland, so that they would be ever mindful of their Scottish roots. But her task was perhaps easier that yours might be in researching, say, a semi-detached villa in Edinburgh or a cottage in Aberdeenshire, because the Grants were proud of their lineage as Highland chieftains and had their family portraits before their eyes to remind them daily of their Scottish and English ancestors.

I think my key piece of advice – which I often offered to researchers in the Record Office – was never expect to find anything at all, and thus the few scraps

Drum Castle.
(NTS)

that might appear in a stray document can only produce considerable gratification, rather than disappointment.

The quickest route to former owners may be through the title deeds to a house and it would be wonderful if these were a complete record of a pattern of ownership. Failing this, at an elementary level a great deal can be gleaned from Post Office and county directories, which were intended to clarify the location of individual and often identically named houses with a cross reference against their (often) similarly named owners. In towns, there are often surprisingly long runs of street directories, whose organisation became ever more sophisticated until overtaken by the modern telephone directories. With street directories you must cross-check the different kinds of entries as the alphabetical lists of persons in one part of the directory may give added information on their professions that is not repeated in the entries arranged by street elsewhere in the directory.

Maps and plans, with the National Library of Scotland's Map Room the expert in the former, and the Scottish Record Office the leading collection of the latter, can reveal surprising degrees of detail. In the Record Office we referred almost daily to copies of General Roy's celebrated military map of 1746, as well as to the published Ordnance Survey Maps. The staff of the Ordnance Survey had to make definitive decisions about the agreed spelling of names – a tricky task in the Gaelic-speaking areas – to codify them for publication on the map. They therefore drew up Parish Name Books, which we can now use to unravel ownerships.

Having identified the people, you can move on, with the help again of the Scottish Record Office, to their testaments and wills – that potentially reveal enormous amounts of telling information and may give vital clues as to where to look next. The sparser records of Births, Marriages and Deaths can clarify many areas of potential confusion. The Census records are a particularly vivid snapshot of the domestic scene in providing details of the family relationships and resident servants.

For an understanding of how a house works, you may be lucky enough to find something as rare as the furniture plans of a Victorian villa in Strathclyde Regional Archives or John Sime's plans for improving his family's flat in the

Haddo House.
(NTS)

Lawnmarket of Edinburgh; but it is much more likely that in trying to understand the way your house may have worked in the past, you will be working from the comparative evidence that has survived by good fortune for houses of similar type.

For years I have been seeking out illustrations of the interiors of Scottish houses and I have tried to fit them into a pattern in my book, *The Scottish Interior*, but there is very little to rub together before the days of photography. Even after that, the range of subjects was limited by established notions of what was thought to be picturesque and by concerns about propriety: thus there are few views of bedrooms, other than those thought to have been occupied by Mary, Queen of Scots, or cottage kitchens excepting that in which Robert Burns was born. A remarkable exception, which I did not know of at the time of writing my book, is the series of record photographs of Haddo House taken by Ishbel, Marchioness of Aberdeen, before the substantial alterations she was to carry out with her husband around 1880. Thankfully, however, in seeking the extraordinary, the photographer was often duped into recording the prosaic for us, as in the photographs of (allegedly) the most haunted house in Scotland, Ballechin, which in themselves are a rare record of a house arranged to be let, and thus with little in the way of family personalia and idiosyncracies.

A key source is provided by inventories of people's possessions – often taken as a result of some kind of disaster. We have just located an undated inventory for Newhailes, which appears to have been drawn up during the 1790s on the death of Lord Hailes. With luck you might get one drawn up by a professional appraiser – at Threave, for example, we have the Rolls Royce of inventories drawn up in 1937 by Jenners, whose precise descriptions of individual objects allow one chair to be distinguished from its neighbour. However, they are often, as at Newhailes, drawn up by trusted household retainers, in this case possibly the housekeeper, and thus display particular knowledge of certain areas, in this case of the textiles. The pioneer scholar of Scottish inventories was John Warrack, who in 1920 published his Rhind Lectures as *Domestic Life in Scotland, 1488-1688* and rather cheekily, but confident in his documentary sources, began with a frontispiece labelled 'Queen Mary's Bedroom (Temp. James VII), Holyrood Place'. To get the most out

Photographs of Lady Katherine Gordon's bedroom *circa* 1877-8 found in a private album belonging to Ishbel Gordon, 7th Countess of Aberdeen. The location of the room is unknown but it is likely that the Countess, who was an accomplished photographer, took the pictures for her own collection.
(RCAHMS)

Caring for the Scottish Interior

of inventories, I would recommend transcribing them, which forces you to concentrate on the unravelling of oddities of handwriting, and then read them again and again, because it usually takes time for things to shake down into a logical place.

Architectural drawings can often be helpful because they render in diagrammatic form a very great deal of information, often showing outlines of existing walls as well as proposed alterations and giving the functions of rooms. In 1995 a large number of us contributed to Rebecca M Bailey's *Scottish Architects Papers*, published by the Royal Incorporation of Architects in Scotland's Rutland Press, which, if you do not know it, may be a source of future pleasure in the discovery.

But the value of such plans, stray photographs and inventories come into their own if you are studying a particular housing type. During the 1980s I was encouraged to study the Edinburgh New Town House by Desmond Hodges of the Edinburgh New Town Conservation Committee. No New Town house today survives entire and unaltered, and with its furniture in situ. However, you can construct a composite house by piecing together archaeological fragments of painted decoration that come to light beneath later wallpapers, alongside the very rare collections of building papers like those for Duncan Campbell of Barcaldine's house at 3 Moray Place and the vivid accounts of their several residences by Elizabeth Grant of Rothiemurchus. The results of such a trawl, which I have singularly failed to reduce to a coherent published form, sadly reveal how very untypical in plan and arrangement is our own Georgian House at 7 Charlotte Square.

Suburban villas are much more difficult to unravel, although there are precious gems like the typebook of Glasgow villas by the architects Boucher and Cousland. I was lucky enough to be able to add this to the National Monuments Records of Scotland.

The accounts of Alexander 'Greek' Thomson's extraordinary Double Villa and Holmwood, which he published in Blackie's *Villa and Cottage Architecture* (1868), nevertheless explain many ordinary practices, like the custom of folding back the solid front door leaves to expose the glass inner door of a vestibule when a family were at home. But villas have always encapsulated people's dreams and are highly individualistic by nature. It was to assist such dreamers that the authors of the many building manuals laboured. There are sadly few specifically Scottish works, but many British publications prove to have strong Scottish connections.

If the first book of Scottish house plans by William Adam, the sumptuous *Vitruvius Scoticus*, depicted houses much grander than most of us can now hope to inhabit, his second, *The Rudiments of Architecture*, with its complicated origins in George Jamiesone's earlier book of 1765, conveys much useful information about house planning in eighteenth-century Scotland. By the nineteenth century there are many more sourcebooks to investigate. The doyen of such journalists was the Scot, John Claudius Loudon, whose *Encyclopaedia of Cottage, Farm and Villa Architecture* (1839) draws on the experience and schemes for dream houses, sent to him by a wide range of correspondents, to allow us to grasp how the average house was organised. John Cornforth was able to draw on these accounts to explain much of what he saw in the early nineteenth-century watercolours of interiors in his *English Interiors 1790–1848* (1978), which revealed the cult of the 'lived-in look', with a scattering of books and magazines and knitting stuffed under a sofa cushion predating the cultivation of such effects by the English National Trust.

An almost scientific interest in the planning and arrangement of houses was a Scottish characteristic, and the master-planner of the British nineteenth-century country house was the Scottish architect William Burn, as Professor David Walker has shown. Many of his ideas can be studied and followed through Robert Kerr's *The Gentleman's House or How to Plan English Residences from the Parsonage to the Palace* (1869), which takes in Balmoral on the way. In planning an ideal dining room, Kerr explains how the architect had not only to allow for the dimensions of the dinner table but also to allow additional space for service by servants around its perimeter. It also had to be correctly orientated to prevent the sun being in the master's eye as he sat in the ideal position in front of the sideboard (from where he could communicate directly with his butler when things failed to go according to carefully laid plans). The art of planning lay in combining the ideal individual characteristics of particular room functions into an overall specification that harmonised the optimum conditions for each type of room within the overall convenience of a design tailored for a particular set of family circumstances in a specific location.

There is a fascinating book, published in Edinburgh in 1869, which draws on Kerr's earlier writings. Entitled *The Grammar of House Planning*, it is principally memorable for the almost algebraic formulas that were used to generate type-plans and thus reveal how Kerr's great mansions were built up aggregatively from individual room units.

Newhailes dining room.
(NTS)

But for turn of the century houses the key is provided by Hermann Muthesius' *The English House*, first published in Germany in 1904-5 which, in spite of its title, includes many Scottish houses and particularly features the work of Charles Rennie Mackintosh. Muthesius was a Prussian civil servant who was sent by his government to study recent British domestic advances, which he studied at a practical level; he and his wife taking a villa, The Priory, in Hampstead. Only a foreigner like Muthesius could perhaps have grasped the essential role of the window cleaner in our national architecture, or charted, with amazement, the prodigal use of fresh flowers on our dining tables. Happily, an English version was published in 1979 and it is perhaps one of those essential books that a student of houses should resolve to read once a year.

Lastly, and still at this level of generality, a great deal can be gleaned from both trade catalogues and the housekeeping manuals aimed at young housewives setting up their first independent married home. There is no general collection of trade material – I tried to buy everything I could when I was at the National Monuments Records of Scotland – but prices were rising all the time and I often missed out. The most complete collection I achieved was of the successive catalogues of William Scot Morton's *Tynecastle Canvas*, a recently conserved example of which is the glory of our new vestibule at 28 Charlotte Square, the Trust's new headquarters. The housekeeping manuals can now be studied to understand the norm rather than to set a standard of acceptability. With their emphasis on containing cost for limited household budgets, these manuals are especially helpful today in identifying distinctions between superficially similar materials.

In conclusion I would urge you again to write your findings down. This has the great benefit of helping to clarify your ideas and to synchronise dates. The result, in future years, might even be as revealing of contemporary taste and ideas as John Marshall's classic account of his Craigmillar villa, Southgate, in his *Amateur House Decoration* (1883) which I was lucky enough to stumble across when I was working on *The Scottish Interior*.

The National Trust for Scotland looks after numerous properties in the nation's interest. Issues of policy for conservation, among other very weighty considerations, come up daily, and the Trust is advised on these matters by expert committees: on collections – the contents; the fabric – buildings; the setting – gardens, pleasure grounds and landscape; and the countryside. Clearly there is overlap and much consultation. These concerns mirror those of any of us looking after our own houses, but the Trust's concerns carry an added weight of explanation: why are properties as they are, how did they get that way, and what value should be placed on them? The Trust carries the extra burden of having to inform visitors of its decisions, as well as carrying them out.

Two Suburban Villas

Bill Brogden

The suburban villa has not enjoyed a particularly positive press in the last century – at least not among critics: the late John Betjeman had a great time poking fun at its pretensions. The same presses, however, extolled the virtues of Ideal Homes. Some of our greatest architects have contributed designs for suburban villas, and they form a very honourable, if not well understood, heritage. The suburban villa stands for much we admire, and its history as an ideal, or type, stretches back to the early eighteenth century.

Admiration for country houses, with contents and setting, attracts most members to the Trust. One of the qualities of the country house is its otherness – my *country* house, as opposed to my house of business, whether urban or rural. Sir John Clerk of Penicuik saw his Mavisbank in those terms and wrote an extended poetic essay on its merits, a genre well established and of which the eighteenth-century daydream poem 'The Choice' is the best known example. This place apart as a repository for ideal life and philosophy appeared early near Edinburgh and later, in the eighteenth century and especially the nineteenth century, also in Glasgow and Aberdeen. The place of retreat for recreation – in earlier times this referred to the spirit or the mind, rather than games or field sport – and for contemplation, began to be known in the eighteenth century as a villa, from *villa di casa* (farmhouse) for simplicity – but also with a good measure of elevated style from the ancient *villa suburbana*, revived in Italy in the sixteenth century.

The National Trust for Scotland has recently acquired two such properties, very different from each other, and also standing as significant turning points. They show the ideals of the suburban villa. Newhailes is an outstanding survival of the eighteenth-century ideal and represents a heritage from Horace and Pliny, and by extension from the very groves of Academe. Holmwood, built some 150 years later, constitutes the *beau ideal* of the Victorian villa and in it are recognisable the qualities

A detail of Arduaine Garden, between Oban and Lochgilphead (*Meconopsis X sheldonii*). (NTS)

The Development of Home and Garden

Editor: Bill Brogden

Newhailes, an essay in extensive gardening.
(NTS)

of modern aspirations as well as those of ancient times. These two emblematic houses, still relatively unknown, can tell us much about the development of the Scottish house and garden. Not only are they comfortably familiar – one in Edinburgh, the other in Glasgow – they were built by and for people such as ourselves: not magnates of great territory, but architects, lawyers and manufacturers.

John Smith built Whitehill, apparently for his own occupation, at the end of the seventeenth century. Just west of Musselburgh, it was (relatively) small and compact, in a form Smith's pupil Colen Campbell would make famous as the villa. Campbell was also the agent for transmitting Smith's collection of drawings by the great Italian architect Andrea Palladio into our common architectural history. Smith's house (a pedimented central section flanked by chambers on three floors) survives as the heart of Newhailes: it established the strong east-west axis that argues for a formal garden setting of parade (or court?) to west and *parterre* (or bowling green) to east. This is supposition, and there may have been related grounds north and south, but the nature and extent of the 'house with gardens and dovecotes and office houses' in 1709 when the Dalrymples acquired it are unknown. The Newhailes (as they renamed it) we have now is essentially their work and reflects the ideals of the second of the Dalrymples, Sir James (1692-1751). The house was significantly enlarged (by whom is unknown, presumably Smith) and set within ambitious, rather crisp, pleasure grounds – no longer a large garden, nor yet a landscape, but what a contemporary called a 'rural and extensive garden' or *ichnographica rustica*. Who its author was remains unknown, although I am tempted to attribute it to the contemporary just quoted, Stephen Switzer. By design, an excluding and idealised 'landscape' is created – very broad and extensive; only topographical features of value are allowed to 'intrude'. All is man-made, but in an early eighteenth-century imitation of nature.

The house and its grounds are closely connected in a variety of ways, giving hospitality with hierarchy, zones for the family, honoured guests, the 'philosophers' – both inside and out, with a sophisticated system of circulation. Simply, the Smith Villa received two wings and a State Suite to the north, reached through a pair of rooms remodelled into a large dining chamber. To the south the balancing wing contained the library – full width and occupying two stories. In the grounds from 1720, symmetry and axial relationships are observed. A short straight drive led directly to the front door in the middle of the new west front, much larger and one side of a handsome enclosed court. Opposite the front door, beyond the reception room and short passage, is the garden, a short plain *parterre*, the same width as the court, flanked by terrace walks and close planted woods. Through it is revealed beyond these, a very broad large plain, essentially empty, with the sea and distant hills beyond its edge. So after a short series of dignified, controlled spaces both internal and external, visitors are presented with a most extensive prospect – as if Edinburgh, Musselburgh and East Lothian have disappeared to be replaced by an ideal nature.

Like other advanced designs of the time, the Newhailes 'garden' – the formal axially-aligned spaces on the garden front – has become an empty recollection of itself. The 'gardens' lie elsewhere and are no longer necessarily formal. To follow the terrace walk east and north a short way reveals either a sort of family garden (seen only from the State Bedroom) whose axis runs parallel to the formal entrance sequence and unites the working parts of Newhailes (and includes most honoured guests) and whose parts recede in reverse hierarchy from visitors. Alternatively the visitor is led on a long and varied walk northwards. The formality or informality of this is open to choice. It is possible to stroll for several miles along well-made terraces with prospect beyond (safely enclosed) pasture to one side and close woodland on the other. At any time a short walk into the woodland would reveal a series of varied small gardens and ornamental buildings with occasional and very surprising views westwards to Arthur's Seat and Edinburgh.

Either or both these modes of appreciating the grounds may be taken and could easily occupy a morning or longer, after rest and food and drink at the Teahouse. It is possible, if arduous, to walk right round the wooded edge of Newhailes – 'the thin gut of woods or enfilade' that Switzer recommended – back to the garden-front door, past extensive woods, both close planted and grove, on the south side. The south facade of Newhailes is more likely to tempt the visitor, because the terrace walk on this side not only forms and embraces the 'garden' but extends westward, and halfway along is what might appear to be a greenhouse – five very tall arched windows. In fact, this is Dalrymple's Library and it was doubtless not only the heart and soul of his house, but of his pleasure grounds as well. Not only could he receive the returning visitor there, but he could easily step through the sash windows onto the terrace and beyond into his philosophers' garden – a formal glade within groves of trees.

Holmwood House, sited to maximise the views and landscape effect by 'concision and borrowing'. (NTS)

The Coupers of Cathcart were as different from the Dalrymples as Glasgow is from Edinburgh, or the nineteenth century from the eighteenth. Robert and James Couper made paper and became rich and prosperous, and as the Dalrymples rose with the first empire boom – the ending of French hegemony, the business of the Union of Parliaments and the South Sea speculation – so the Coupers prospered from the second empire boom, as suppliers of stationery to the Government during and following the Crimean War. Their mills are on the White Cart, a tributary of the upper Clyde, and on the ground above it to the south and west the brothers built two villas – Sunnyside and Holmwood. Their site was wooded and dramatic, and appealed to the taste of those, bred on the picturesque, who had formed an appreciation of the Clyde for its pictorial and associational qualities. They were able to enjoy both the visual and business aspects of their site; living above the mill, out of sight but close at hand. Their site was empty but had the benefit of the wooded slopes on the east and north sides of the river.

Holmwood was sited at the extreme southern edge of its limited site, so as to maximise the views at its disposal: the garden grounds immediately to the north; the wooded banks of the river encircling it; Glasgow with its 'picturesque' bustle; and of course the Clyde, in its various aspects; the hills north of the city; and finally Ben Lomond – all play significant roles in Holmwood's 'landscape'. Sunnyside no longer exists, and Alexander Thomson's design for its neighbour Holmwood ignores it, or perhaps, relegates its baronial form to one of a number of objects in landscape. Thomson worked for the younger brother, James Couper (1818–77), whose plot is further uphill from the mill.

If Newhailes is an essay in extensive gardening then Holmwood achieves landscape effects by concision and by borrowing. Thomson's method seems to follow the advice of J C Loudon, the great Scottish encyclopedist of arboriculture agriculture, gardening and villadom – especially in his *Encyclopaedia of Cottage Farm and Villa Architecture*. Loudon's way was to observe meticulously the setting of the proposed villa, noting horizons, views, objects and opportunities. Switzer had recommended the same but Loudon takes it step by step, and might have been describing the as yet unbuilt Holmwood. Thomson founds Holmwood at the most

Investigating the grounds of Holmwood House.
(NTS)

advantageous place to appreciate (command) its landscape. This spot is realised as an exquisite circular temple – whose columns stand distinct and beyond the glazed screen, engaged at the end of one of the three reception rooms. Thus he provides a panorama of over 200° of landscaped grounds (small, admittedly, but landscape for all that) ornamented by appropriately scaled trees and shrubs chosen for their habit, colours and 'architectural' qualities and disposed with art, to be best viewed from the parlour window. Everything beyond this is outside Holmwood's landscape, but is yet very intimately part of it. If the owner was master of only a small space he eagerly appropriated all that lay outside.

The house is as much part of the landscape composition as an object itself. It is first and best glimpsed foreshortened and to the side, with the circular temple feature furthest away, behind and to the side of which mass low gables, with sharp spreading eaves. An echo of the temple tops the whole as cupola/skylight while extensive garden walls grow out of the villa composition towards the entry gate, where the whole is restated in miniature. Holmwood's link to our time is particularly to the numerous bungalows and villas of Scotland built early in the twentieth century, with their formal bay windows giving views of tightly composed groups of plants, and some part of our collective landscape lying beyond.

Like Newhailes, Holmwood celebrates its links to antiquity, but by means that make it more accessible to modern eyes. The villa (indistinguishable from its grounds) is 'at once classic and picturesque'. It has the same qualities of object, of composition and detail, and relation of building and landscape, that are so admired in the work of Frank Lloyd Wright or Bernard Maybeck in America; and as Thomson shared these attitudes to antiquity and landscape with his contemporary, the German K F Shinkel, so too did Mies Van der Rohe. Holmwood looks forward to our times as much as it does backward to Newhailes.

As part of the National Trust's duty to explain its actions we have become concerned to identify and bring into practice the very best in conservation theory. Like our colleagues in museum work we have subscribed to the idea of conserve as found, and to some extent this notion has the imprimatur of international agreements such as the Burra Charter. With furniture and objects of art we feel ourselves bound to treat the objects with the greatest possible respect, and restoration is almost never attempted. It is possible, and sometimes very instructive, to isolate fragments of wall-covering, or bits of upholstery hanging on by its last threads, and to conserve these and present them as a natural part of the ageing that all buildings and their contents go through. But what of grounds – gardens and landscapes – made up of living things? One can no more conserve a tree as found than hold one's breath. Yet the same principle applies: the design, whether an artful assemblage of plants, or architectural wherein plants play a structural and supporting role, has to be protected, enhanced, and perhaps re-presented. Just how this can be achieved in practice is a significant part of Duncan Donald's lively chapter on the impact of visitors on National Trust Properties.

Up the Garden Path:
The Impact of Visitors
on the National Trust for Scotland Gardens

Duncan Donald

I realise that I am a stranger amongst thieves, but I must start by contending that, except as a result of conscious human intervention or an Act of God, buildings and their contents change relatively slowly. Consider an average room, let us say the great Gallery at Fyvie Castle. The photograph here might have been taken twenty years ago, but the chances are, should you visit tomorrow, that most of the elements shown will be in the same place, in much the same condition. They will have been dusted and polished from time to time but, if they have been moved elsewhere, this will probably be a conscious decision of one of my curatorial or property colleagues. Whenever the photograph was taken, however, the one thing sure to change within a day or two is the arrangement of fresh-cut flowers prominently displayed on the centre table. That is the interface with which we gardeners continually deal: the daily struggle of life and death.

The Gallery at Fyvie Castle.
(NTS)

By their very nature, gardens are living, dynamic, continually changing works of art. That is why so many people enjoy going outside from their sedentary home environments to relax in their gardens. It is also what makes them such an important component in many National Trust for Scotland properties. The liveliness and interest of ornamental gardens explains why so many former owners developed them, often at huge ongoing expense, as fitting settings in which to show off their buildings, to entertain their chums and swank to their houseguests. It is why many present-day visitors will often pay repeat visits to a garden property – to see it in different seasons, at different times of day, in different years – in a way that, I would suggest, they are much less likely to do for the houses or castles themselves. I have heard the recent spate of television garden makeover programmes, such as *Ground Force*, described as 'imitations' of the 'indoor' versions, such as *Changing Rooms*. However, while it is true that some of these programmes have given indoor designers the (to me, unwelcome) chance to bring their paint-boxes and floorboards outside, the truth is that it is really the other way round. Gardens have always been changeable in the short-term; it is the indoor makeover which is art imitating nature, in order to try to compete in interest.

The most obvious features of this change in gardens are the plants themselves: our living works of art are made up of components that are mortal. Some – annuals – we know will only last for one year – others such as yew trees – with appropriate management, may last for more than a millennium. Where we place them and how we use them in our work of art will depend on our, often subliminal, judgement of their longevity. A plant's longevity is a characteristic of its type which has remained largely constant throughout its history in cultivation: be it an annual or a yew, it will have performed more or less the same at whatever period of history in which it was planted. However, as Bill Brogden has already shown, history and fashion have also provided another major dynamic for change in gardens, influencing the availability of particular plants and the ways in which they have been grown and displayed.

I must also mention in passing two other forces for change which add instability to our living works of art: change of staff is an accelerating problem in an increasingly mobile and restless society; and environmental change, be it on the global or the microcosmic scale, can also have profound effects. (Will you still grow apples if global warming allows Aberdeenshire to grow peaches and pomegranates?)

However, the catalyst of instability on which I am concentrating in this chapter is that of visitor pressure.

There is no question that, from a conservation viewpoint, one of the most damaging events ever to afflict a garden could, potentially, be its acquisition by the National Trust for Scotland. I say this not to betray my employer, nor to belittle the superb efforts of so many of my colleagues in the magnificent work they do to maintain national treasures that, without the Trust, might well have faced a rapid slide into dereliction or even total loss. However, the moment of preservation through acquisition has usually only a short-term effect. After that come two things: first, the need for active intervention to slow, or channel, undesirable change – in other words, conservation rather than preservation; and second, the need, inherent in the Trust's schizophrenic nature, for public access, on the basis that we do what we do 'for the benefit of the nation'. That generally means letting – *ie* encouraging – the public to come and visit. These two factors can often co-exist if handled sympathetically, but equally, as we shall see, they can conflict with one another.

The first garden that the Trust accepted as a feature in its own right, rather than as a mere adjunct to an important building, was Inverewe. By the time of its acquisition in 1952, it was already attracting some 3000 visitors a year; today it attracts between 120,000 and 150,000, and is thus a major stimulus for tourism in an otherwise remote area. Perhaps inevitably, the impact of such enormously increased admissions has led to design changes. Dawn Macleod – the donor, Mairi Sawyer's 'adopted niece' – wrote critically in 1990 (in *Hortus*, No 15) of how, by 1962, already 'alterations had begun to obliterate the wayward signatures of Osgood [Mackenzie] and his daughter Mairi in favour of a more standardised "Trustmark"'. Mrs Macleod articulated succinctly some of the chief problems we face – pressure of numbers propels design changes, which can themselves be seen to be changing the very spirit of the place we claim to be conserving. In her words:

> … *hundreds of weight-bearing feet do require wider, firmer parade grounds: but this woodland garden wasn't designed to accommodate armies on the march. There is the rub. It may be that real conservation implies some restriction in numbers, and that this point deserves serious debate within the council chambers of National Trusts.*

In particular she singled out the change to the garden's entrance, where a sloping daffodil-filled lawn had been replaced with a visitor-centre complex; the 'intrusions' of year-round drive-side planting and a Crathes-style herbaceous border near the house; and a 'mechanical tailoring' or over-tidying by, implicitly, too many professional staff who, she clearly felt, 'might benefit from a manual entitled *How to keep a Garden under control while giving the Impression that it is a work of Nature*'.

Pressure of feet can very soon lead to destruction of turf or soft-bottomed paths. My predecessor saw the conversion of turf paths in Crathes' walled garden to Yorkstone slabs; and by constant re-turfing, we continue to fight to retain the essential quality of greenness of the grass paths at Branklyn, despite its 20,000 visitors per year. The 1992 acquisition Arduaine Garden, between Oban and Lochgilphead, has shown a leap in numbers as did Inverewe: from 3000 per year over a three-month opening season under private ownership in 1991, to more than

Arduaine Garden, azaleas.
Arduaine's path system is coping with increased visitor numbers.
(NTS)

20,000 per year from year-round opening under NTS ownership. Here, I should argue, the effect of that seven-fold increase on the garden's design has been minimal, because the path system we inherited was already good and remains capable of handling even larger numbers without strain.

However, visitors have other needs as well as good path systems by which to navigate. At Arduaine we have built a modest toilet-block but, with a major hotel on the garden's doorstep, we have been able to resist the pressure to provide catering on site. Not so at Culzean, where 300,000 visitors per year have necessitated the building of carparks and restaurants, and the opportunity has been taken to add several shops and two plant sales areas – all a far cry from the days when the Earls of Cassilis twice moved the public road further away from the castle so that they could enjoy their picturesque designed landscape in private. Culzean's landscape was most certainly not designed with the concept of one-third of a million visitors a year, so incorporating features such as coach parks needs to be done with some sensitivity.

As my quotations from Dawn Macleod show, there can also be pressure to alter the planting to accommodate visitors. This may be a direct effect of the pressure of feet, which we have already considered, and it may operate on the level of the individual plant. People will beat a path to the so-called giant rhubarb (*Gunnera manicata*) to have their photograph taken under its enormous towering leaves – so it's no good thinking that you will win by hiding it away at the back of the border; you might as well bow to the inevitable and plant it prominently with, in the wet ground that it enjoys, a carefully positioned stone slab on which the model can pose. Other individual specimens (*eg Metrosideros umbellatus* beside the Inverewe Drive) can be so photogenic at the appropriate season that you need to anticipate the photographers' ring that will develop round them. Some good all-year-round plants, the maple *Acer griseum* for example, can become hackneyed through over-use; we can avoid this to some extent by being more discriminatory in following thematic plantings – especially historically accurate planting, which often also accords with our evaluation and subsequent conservation of key significant periods within a particular garden's development. Perhaps most difficult of all are the plants that, though inappropriate or past their sell-by date, become firm favourites of our visitors and sacred cows that cannot be slain without risk of a furore. I could evidence several notable old Aberdeenshire trees – the horse chestnut at Crathes, the sycamore at Drum – which, because their fate was to grow too close to highly visited major buildings, have simply had to be taken down on safety grounds before they fell on someone.

However, as Dawn Macleod pointed out when fulminating against the drive-side planting and the herbaceous border in front of the house at Inverewe, it may be whole borders that are changed, even whole gardens created – as at Priorwood – in order to attract and satisfy visitors. Part of this is due to the pressure, under Trust management, for year-round opening. Malleny Garden, in private hands, was noted for its displays of sweet peas and half-hardy annuals; these were spectacular for a few weeks each summer. Under the pressure of year-round opening, my predecessor Eric Robson worked with the present Head Gardener to substitute a mixed border with much longer appeal. Consider also the Falkland delphiniums. Percy Cane, whose garden (designed around 1950) we are principally conserving there nowadays, had Russell lupins along one particular border. In time the ground developed a replant disorder, and became lupin-sick, with the result that the Trust decided to rest it by replacing the lupins with delphiniums for a few years, before – and this was always the intention – reintroducing the lupins again. The inevitable happened

Malleny Garden, where all-year opening is encouraged through the development of a mixed border. (NTS)

The Development of Home and Garden

and visitors took to the magnificent display of delphiniums, to the point that horror is now expressed locally at the suggestion that they should be replaced with *lupins* – regardless of the fact that Percy Cane's design, which is what we are actually conserving, simply didn't include our beautiful tall blue monsters.

Gardens inevitably change; the important question here is what is most significant, what should be conserved? – and what therefore, by default, can be allowed to be changed? Gardens are works of art intended to be seen, and public acclaim must, naturally, be part of the equation – but, if the Trust's role is to mean anything, it can only be a part; we also need to protect inherited significance. I would suggest that this is actually most important, and most difficult, when public taste changes, as in the fashion for growing lupins. If we are not to protect them, who will, and where will they be found when the fashion changes back and they become 'period' plants worthy of a historic planting?

Having people around probably acts as a better deterrent against theft than their absence, and in that respect private properties might at first seem more vulnerable than Trust ones. However, in opening up a garden's gates to the general public, there is a greater risk of admitting that small proportion intent on sizing up the joint and coming back later to remove what they want. Authentic 'period' garden ornaments have always been expensive, but there has been a dramatic escalation of prices of even the more ordinary items, associated with highly successful sales days run by leading auction houses during the 1970s and 80s. We, opening for the public benefit, often go out of our way, through interpretation on the ground or in guidebooks, to highlight the special features of our estates; we stop short of putting valuations on them, but the effect must be similar. Nowadays we do need to think quite carefully about siting; about security devices and the like. Over the past few years I have drawn attention to this particular problem by illustrating it with a photograph of the statue of 'Paris', then in a vulnerable position at Fyvie. I hope that this was not the reason that someone did indeed try, in dead of night, to remove the statue, albeit unsuccessfully!

In the case of a few very rare plants, we have even taken to making sure that they are not labelled. Thus we ensure that their theft, if it occurs, would be limited to the few experts who recognise the plant itself, rather than the larger number who might deduce its rarity from the unfamiliarity of its name. One also learns, sadly, to avoid putting out, labelled, into public areas, plants that are literally irreplaceable – unless there is a reserve stock safely behind the scenes or shared with another garden.

On the subject of labelling, plant labels also get stolen. To give one impression of the scale of the problem, a recently labelled 'trail' at Inverewe lost 100 of its 300 labels within the first year; the cost of replacing these, in labour and materials, is not insignificant. When I ran a botanic garden the only definition that seemed to cover the many disparate sites that operated world-wide under that title was 'a garden that is open to the public and where the plants are generally labelled'. It seems to be the accepted standard, no matter how historically 'authentic' the rest of one of our garden restorations is, that there should be some form of interpretation on site and ideally the plants will be labelled, so that visitors can learn what they are and, if they wish, acquire them themselves. Maintaining a labelled collection is itself a major undertaking, involving, these days, the need for careful mapping and computerised records systems – again partly to satisfy an external demand for information about what Trust gardens grow.

Labels are only one aspect of garden interpretation. We might also require pre-directional signs so that our visitors find the garden in the first place; internal

Falkland Palace Gardens, delphiniums.
(NTS)

directional signs so that they can navigate their way around (it is not just in Hampton Court Maze but in some of our larger gardens too, that, without help, people can genuinely get lost and give themselves a fright as to how they are ever going to find their way out again); border or area signs to explain what we are displaying; guidebooks; audio 'wands'; laminated 'bats' ... and garden staffs trained to lead guided tours or to keep working while giving succinct information to assist casual visitor enquiries.

In conclusion, we are indeed fortunate that, compared with our sister organisation the National Trust for England and Wales, our garden visitor numbers generally operate in the 20,000-40,000 band; theirs are on average at least double that. None of our gardens has yet faced the need for stringent visitor control – via, for example, 'de-advertising' or timed ticketing – that our buildings at Craigievar and Crathes Castles and the Hill House have. The problems so far remain more those of inadequate surfacing – and I do not think that we have yet discovered a wholly acceptable solution to this – and of an accrual of minor damage resulting from excessive visitor numbers; and of the subtle but pervasive pressure to stay 'children of our time' and use contemporary planting and methods of interpretation.

However, I must counterbalance what I have been saying so far by acknowledging that, despite appearances sometimes, we do like having visitors in Trust gardens. This chapter was intended to highlight the conflicts that can arise between conservation and accessibility, and naturally I have chosen my examples to show this. All that we do, we do for 'the benefit of the nation'. We welcome visitors; we need them to pay their admission or subscription; we want them to enjoy what we have to show them; and ideally they will also support our work further by buying from our plant sales areas (and carefully sited shops and tearooms) before they leave. On the subject of fund-raising, I also pay tribute to the support we receive from Scotland's Gardens Scheme: the Gardens Fund of the Trust is one of the principal beneficiaries of the Scheme, under which private gardens open throughout Scotland. Many of our garden properties hold events, and those held under the auspices of the SGS bring in visitors who have a clear interest in gardens and gardening.

At the end of the day, we gardeners have much in common with colleagues from other disciplines. While access and conservation can often go hand in hand, visitor pressure – if not controlled properly – can lead to harmful changes to the very thing we are trying to conserve. The challenge to us is to promote the former successfully while not jeopardising the latter.

Not only does the pressure of visitor numbers have a significant impact on how the Trust looks after and displays its gardens, but the identity of the garden has to be taken into account. Many of the gardens the Trust has inherited are the individual efforts of committed and skilful gardener-designers. These inspired makers never stopped in their search for the perfect plant in its perfect place, in concert with the garden as a whole. Not only are such gardens essentially individual efforts, they require constant care of the same kind, and that is what the Trust finds so difficult to continue: committed professional staff advised by a committee of experts do not make quirky and highly individual statements in gardens. How to 'preserve' or continue to develop such gardens is one of our prevailing problems in establishing a theory for conservation. In debating such ideas, the availability and the appropriateness of plant choice is often an issue. Generally a structure of 'happy natives' – which includes established exotics – with happily acclimatised introductions is preferred, and Nicola Singleton shows how such plants might be sourced from Scottish nurseries, not only for Trust gardens but for private ones as well.

Inverewe Garden pond.
(NTS)

The Development of Home and Garden

Scottish Plants, Availability and Sourcing

Nicola Singleton

Branklyn Garden plant sale.
(NTS)

Castle Fraser, an east-coast garden with a herbaceous border.
(NTS)

The range of garden plants available to us today is vast compared to 40 years ago. In those days there were no plants grown in containers; most of them were grown in the soil, dug up in autumn and sold as bare-root plants. This system meant that plants were only available in autumn and early winter, and garden centres were unheard of. With the introduction of stronger and cheaper plastics, plants began to be grown in plastic pots. This was a major breakthrough in the horticultural world because it meant that plants could be sold all year round, and signalled the real beginning of the plant sales trade. Many growers were happy to move away from their original production of crops requiring heat, like tomatoes and chrysanthemums, because of the escalating price of oil, and to diversify into producing garden plants in pots. Hardy plant production meant much smaller heating bills.

With the increase in availability of plants, nurseries began to develop in various locations in Scotland. If the nursery was located near a large population centre it usually began supplying direct to the public. However the best soils and climates for growing in Scotland are not generally near well-populated areas; Argyll is an example. These nurseries, located in more remote parts of the country, had to develop their production for the wholesale market. Over the years Scotland has developed a reputation for quality, hardy plants. The range of plants available from Scottish nurseries is much wider than you might think, with ornamental plant production in Scotland accounting for over £80 million of business a year. Shrubs, conifers and herbaceous plants are all grown throughout the country, but, to be more specific, nurseries around Inverness produce almost half of the country's wildflowers, herbaceous plants and herbs, while many of Scotland's roses are grown in Fife, Ayrshire and Aberdeen. The west coast is well known for a wide range of plants including climbing plants, and the area around the Clyde Valley is recognised for its bedding plant production. We only have to start looking further afield when trying to source large mature plants or less hardy plants like tree ferns or clipped bay trees. Many of these are imported from Europe.

Scotland also has a lot of specialist growers who run small nurseries, mainly through mail order. The types of plants they grow are usually difficult to produce in large numbers, so they don't supply in wholesale quantities but advertise and sell through specialist gardening magazines or their own catalogues. These plants are always in demand because they are relatively uncommon. Many new or unusual plants are only initially available in small numbers. These are often plants that have been grown from seed sourced abroad, in China or in the Himalayas, for example. A number of Scottish horticulturists regularly go abroad to look for new species of plants with garden value or to collect seed. As with the plant hunters of old, many new species of alpine plants have been introduced in this way. Rhododendrons are another group of plants that is being collected or bred. They are prized commercially because they are very popular with gardeners and can be difficult to propagate. Some of the best-known varieties of hardy azaleas and rhododendrons now available for sale were collected and bred by a well-known Scottish grower. Plant collecting helps to increase the range and types of plants available for gardens.

It also helps reduce the risk of extinction faced by certain plants whose natural habitat is under threat.

Most new species or varieties of plants are grown and trialled for many years before they become available to the public. The trials are carried out to look at different traits, for example, to see how the plants perform under different growing conditions, how well they flower and how disease resistant they are. They may never get as far as becoming garden plants, but they might be used in breeding if they have beneficial characteristics like a late flowering period.

The biggest factor affecting what Scottish nurseries produce is climate, because of the two distinct weather patterns on the east and west of the country. What grows in Argyll may not grow in Aberdeen. This difference is partly caused by the Gulf Stream running up the west coast and creating overall milder and wetter conditions than in the east. These warmer conditions are ideal for plants like rhododendrons and evergreen shrubs, while the cooler, dry conditions in the east favour alpine plants. If you travel around Scotland visiting nurseries, you will find that, unlike the south of England where there is a nursery every hundred yards, Scottish nurseries tend to be grouped together. Argyll is home to a number of heather, shrub and rhododendron nurseries along with many of the most successful propagation nurseries in Scotland. The favourable climate makes it easier to produce good quality uniform plants in a short space of time. Many of these plants end up being supplied to English nurseries as well as Scottish. Heathers and rhododendrons are well-known examples of west-coast plants but more exotic plants like the Himalayan blue poppy (*Meconopsis betonicifolia*), the Chilean fire bush (*Embothrium coccineum*) and the lantern tree (*Crinodendron hookerianum*) are all specialities of the area. They often grow better there than they do in the south. The cooler, drier east is home to a number of alpine and herbaceous nurseries. These plants prefer low humidity and often won't grow if their foliage is constantly wet. Their leaves die away in the winter so they can tolerate low temperatures.

Over the last ten years the popularity of alpines and herbaceous plants has escalated, whereas in the 1980s conifers and heathers were the height of fashion. The former are hardy and grow reliably every year. Many new varieties are brought out each year to satisfy demand. Ferns, grasses and bamboo are starting to emerge as the latest desirable plants and many Scottish growers are adding these to their range.

The overriding attribute of the plants available in Scotland is quality. I spend a lot of time sourcing plants and visiting growers, and the nursery trade is constantly striving to maintain its quality. The nurseries that thrive keep up with modern developments and produce plants which suit their climate.

The nursery industry is enjoying a boom at present with constant coverage in magazines and on television and radio. Gardening is a fashionable occupation and people with more leisure time are looking to their gardens as an extra room. With the huge range of plants available and with plants being bred for hardiness, flower colour, scent and even shape, the new varieties on the market will perform well. The importance of the garden to the house must not be underestimated, and a well-stocked garden can often significantly increase the value of a house to a potential buyer.

This is simply an introduction to some of the work that goes on in Scottish horticulture. There is a thriving industry in this country, responsible for producing a huge variety of plants, many of which end up growing in our gardens. By creating beautiful gardens in conjunction with Scottish homes we can contribute to a better living environment.

Culzean fire bush.
(NTS)

Brodick Castle Garden. An example of a west-coast garden showing the types of plants that grow well there, such as *Primula* and *Gunnera manicata*.
(NTS)

The Development of Home and Garden

Plants	Nursery Supplier
Herbaceous plants, wildflowers and herbs	*Highland Liliums* Kiltarlity, by Beauly, Inverness-shire
Herbs	*Brin Herb Nursery* Brin School Fields, Flichity, Inverness
Roses	*J Cocker & Sons,* Whitemyres, Lang Stracht, Aberdeen
	John Train & Sons Benston, Station Rd, Tarbolton, Ayr
	R C Ferguson & Sons Sands Rose Nurseries, Kincardine on Forth, Fife
Rhododendrons	*Braevallich Nursery* Braevallich Farm, by Dalmally, Argyll
Heathers	*Inverliever Nursery* Ford, Lochgilphead, Argyll
Bedding plants	*Trotterbank Nursery* Rowanbank, Overtown, Wishaw
	J & C Scott Meadowside Nursery, Lanark Road Braidwood, Carluke
Specialist alpine nursery	*Christie's Nursery* Downfield, Westmuir, Angus
Rhododendrons/Azaleas	*Glendoick Gardens Ltd* Glendoick, Perth
Plant liners (young plants)	*Craignish Nursery* Ardfearn, by Lochgilphead, Argyll
	Skipness Plants The Gardens, Skipness, nr Tarbert, Argyll
Alpines (gentians)	*Angus Heathers* Crosston Farm, Letham, Forfar, Angus.
Herbaceous plants (ferns and grasses)	*Greens Nursery* New Fleenas Farm Nairn

Haddo House rose garden.
(NTS)

The above list comprises a cross-section of wholesale nurseries located throughout Scotland. Their locations illustrate where certain types of plants will naturally grow best. However, climatic conditions can be manipulated by growing plants in glasshouses or polythene tunnels.

They are generally not open to the public, but do supply the numerous plant retail outlets scattered across Scotland.

The Future of Scottish Homes

Professor Andrew MacMillan

Self-image is important to individuals and to nations, and buildings and towns that are persisting elements in a nation's mythic landscape must be of prime importance in establishing a sense of national identity. Hence the question of the future of the Scottish home: is there a Scottish home, has it a future? Where does it fit in with 'A Policy For Architecture'? We all have those tourist images in our mind: the sea girt Hebridean house; the but and ben; the medieval castle; the Adam country seat; Edinburgh's New Town; Glasgow's tenements and Victorian villas; Easterhouse and the Red Road flats. In their own way all Scottish, all firmly located in space and in time, creating a continuum of changing lifestyles, of futures fulfilled, of old eras outworn. So what of today and tomorrow in a nation intent on reasserting its difference, in an era of global culture, in a potentially federated island?

There can only be a Scottish home as long as there is a Scottish lifestyle, and as long as we value our heritage and living traditions. But it will be a matter of how we live or wish to live today, rather than of style or stone. In one area at least, its future seems reasonably safe: that of the inner-city home of wrinklies and the mobile young; perhaps more accurately the upwardly mobile young, who value proximity to entertainment, the arts and eating out, and hold socialising as a priority; and also and most importantly, of the owner and occupier clients of the Housing Associations, who value, in addition, proximity to work and shopping.

Its future in the countryside and in smaller country towns is less certain. In the outer suburbs and the commuter belts it is bleak. There it is under immense pressure from the conventional image of cosy 'middle England'. Avidly pushed by the profit driven media, television and newspaper home supplements in particular, this image constitutes a genuine risk that any distinctive Scottish lifestyle will not only disappear, but that the city itself will be infected by interventions such as inner-city business parks designed to delude commuters that they have never left their safe suburban environment. Thus the answer to the question about the future of the Scottish home is problematic.

Edinburgh's New Town, Glasgow's West End and its Merchant City are strongholds of the Scottish urban tradition of low rise, high-density living. They suggest, along with our devolved parliament, that a strong sense of being different does exist in Scotland: an awareness of a separate identity and of possessing different social values from other parts of Britain. That this is widespread is particularly instanced by the activities and achievements of the Housing Associations whose grass-roots management of existing city building stock includes renovation and alteration to modernise what is clearly seen to be a desirable building type, and also the commissioning of innovative architects to design modern versions. These architects are briefed to incorporate twenty-first century necessities, which include central heating, sustainability, attention to the needs of car users, and balconies to enjoy outdoor life, or personal planting. All this adds up to a desire to support the traditional dense amenity-friendly city lifestyle and savour the civilised advantages it offers.

Low rise, high-density tenement living is European, has had at least 2000

A standard 'kit' house, Gruinard, Inverness-shire.
(BENJAMIN TINDALL ARCHITECTS)

The romantic image of the tenement,
Lawnmarket, Edinburgh, 1896.
(BEN TINDALL)

years of development to reach its present condition and continues to be versatile and responsive to urban needs, capable of catering for rich and poor, married and single, providing large or small accommodation in a way no other building type does. It supports Scotland's constructive attitude to and stronger cultural links with Europe. Scotland benefits from explorations of modern tenement possibilities in Spain, the Netherlands, Germany, where contemporary solutions are proliferating. Innovative exhibitions (like the Housing on the Green in Glasgow '99) and new developments like the Maryhill Association's 21st century's tenement competition and the Reidvale Housing Association's Graham Square development offer a preview now of what the future of the urban Scottish home might be like. So the tenement at last is in safe hands and seems certain to continue to play its part in shaping the Scottish character in and of our towns and cities, and continuing to provide a unique lifestyle-supporting habitat in the United Kingdom.

So what of the suburban and the rural house? The early suburbs were a flight from the impact of the industrial revolution on our towns. Overcrowded, insanitary, soot and disease ridden, towns presented a noxious microclimate from which the new wealth fled first by carriage, then by rail, bus and tram and finally with the freedom conferred by the private car. Now that industry has largely gone from the cities, they are becoming re-inhabitable for a variety of reasons, but the suburbs, and indeed rural areas, have been invaded by a new threat, the commodification of 'the house'. The original leafy suburbs, carriage generated, with relatively well-off inhabitants, are Scottish in their substantial stone villas, traditionally built and set in spacious gardens; an adjunct to the town rather than a substitute. They are now under threat through the random development of isolated sites, building in the gardens, or replacing the existing villa with a set of housebuilder units, houses or flats. The architectural integrity of the suburb is lost. The increase in density is seldom accompanied by any corresponding increase in amenity, hence an increasingly negative car impact on roads and existing city centres.

Where the older suburbs had been sensitively sited in relation to their countryside situation, newer residential developments treat the site merely as a repository for housing units, these a purchased commodity, saleable anywhere, largely in the hands of large national housebuilders. Commodified mass-produced housebuilder units further mitigate against any sense of place and hence identity, and place stresses on the existing city centres both by increases in traffic and parking provision and, through out of town shopping malls, eroding the variety of city shopping provision. That these 'estate' developments are the outcome of a mass housebuilders' market inevitably means that regional variety is reduced, that national (*ie* London) values predominate: witness the proliferation of half-timbered and Cotswold-type 'collages' which have appeared in Scotland in the last ten years. Existing topographic features, landscape, shelter planting, watercourses, or ponds are largely ignored to maximise return on site purchase. Modern earth-moving machinery effortlessly removes any feature that reduces unit numbers, but might impart individuality. Product advertising for the national UK market removes any real reference to the actual site, being the first stage in the depersonalisation of the habitat, and the earthworks compound this in removing any sense of place.

The 'image' of the houses or 'homes' tends to be that of a cosy 'middle England' family – Mum, Dad, two children and a floppy dog to unroll the toilet paper. This unreal image in a reality of an increasing majority of single parent families, many in straitened circumstances, is widely advertised, aided and abetted by imported Australian and American soaps, and is both pernicious and socially divisive and presents problems which urgently need addressing. That suburbia will continue to exist is certain; that it will be Scottish is most unlikely; that it also has a deleterious effect on the rural house is increasingly obvious – nothing will demean our Scottish landscape real or 'mythic', more than a blatantly anglicised kit house in a prominent position. To understand this, visualise it in a Colin Baxter context. How then, to answer the question?

In the urban centres a visibly Scottish lifestyle seems likely to continue to be desirable, the advantages of inner-city living becoming increasingly clear as the deleterious effects of heavy industry and solid fuel fires disappear. It also becomes possible to re-green the city – witness the new trees in Buchanan Street in Glasgow. The tenement, the urban type which has exported itself to resort and country towns, and can be said to characterise Scottish towns, is undergoing creative rethinking and modernisation both by private developers and by semi-public Housing Associations and will probably continue to exist as a distinctively Scottish home.

The commuter suburbs, however, are seriously at risk of becoming depersonalised, modulated by fiscal rather than societal parameters. Depersonalisation and social divisiveness are genuine risks, unless housing investigation now addresses the problems of the suburb in the same depth as it has that of the tenement. There may be a 'real life' relationship developing between historic urban centre as social meeting place and suburban housing-only ghettos, but the aspects of 'Scottish' identity and social association need a deeper study if eventual alienation is to be avoided. Gated and armed guarded enclaves are one possible nightmare future if this trend continues. A promising aspect of suburban development being examined elsewhere in Europe, and a little in London, is the use of a villa typology to house groups of families enjoying communal open space, and parking (in the best examples, under the villa). This can usefully densify an area to the extent of supporting some local amenities, and permits a more architectural approach to the buildings themselves. Higher densities of development facilitate social interaction, amenity provision, and less use of the car (for the school run, or the sports centre ditto). But the number of problems in the suburbs which are not being addressed make a future for a distinctive Scottish suburban home less likely. Homes, perhaps; enclaves, yes; social problems, undoubtedly.

So far the architectural profession has tended to wash its hands of the suburb, perhaps unable to resist the financial weight of the national housebuilders. Now is the time in Scotland to find out if the Policy for Architecture can influence the biggest use of resources in land, in roads and in transport and investment, in a less formal-looking sector of the economy – in other words, can the Policy address and hope to influence the housebuilder market? After that to consider the rural home as a Scottish but modern object in a Scottish landscape should be easy.

New housing in the countryside, sensitive to culture and sustainability.
(BARRA & VATERSAY HOUSING ASSOCIATION, BENJAMIN TINDALL ARCHITECTS)

The realisation of the image of the 'sea girt' house, Craobh Haven, Argyll.
(BEN TINDALL)

The Development of Home and Garden

Sourcing Traditional Materials and Skill Requirements
for the Repair of Scotland's Domestic Architecture

The Care and Conservation of Georgian Houses: A Maintenance Manual, Architectural Press and Edinburgh New Town Conservation Committee (ENTCC) (London 1980).

Conservation Manual, 15 sections, Glasgow West Conservation Trust (Glasgow 1991-9).

The Repair of Historic Buildings in Scotland, Historic Scotland Technical Conservation Research and Education (TCRE) Division (Edinburgh 1995).

Conference Proceedings – The Historic Scotland International Lime Conference, Historic Scotland TCRE Division (Edinburgh 1996).

Conference Proceedings – Historic Scotland Traditional Building Materials Conference, Historic Scotland TCRE Division (Edinburgh 1997).

Case studies of Traditional Lime Harling – A Discussion Document, Historic Scotland TCRE Division (Edinburgh 1996).

A Future for Stone in Scotland, Historic Scotland TCRE Division (Edinburgh 1997).

The Conservation and Conversion of Rural Buildings in the Lothians: Practitioners Guide, Historic Scotland TCRE Division (Edinburgh 2000).

Old Schoolhouse, Cottown, Historic Scotland TCRE Division, pending (Edinburgh 2001).

Preparation and use of Lime Mortars: Technical Advice Note (TAN) 1, Historic Scotland TCRE Division (Edinburgh 1995).

Thatches and Thatching Techniques: TAN 4, Historic Scotland TCRE Division (Edinburgh 1996).

The Hebridean Blackhouse: TAN 5, Historic Scotland TCRE Division (Edinburgh 1996).

Earth Structures in Scotland: TAN 6, Historic Scotland TCRE Division (Edinburgh 1996).

Quarries of Scotland: TAN 12, Historic Scotland TCRE Division (Edinburgh 1997).

The Archaeology of Scottish Thatch: TAN 13, Historic Scotland TCRE Division (Edinburgh 1998).

COST Action C5, 'Urban Heritage – Building Maintenance', Draft Report, European Commission, unpublished (Brussels 1999).

Construction Employment and Training Forecast 2000-2004, Construction Industry Training Board Research Document (Bircham Newton, October 1999).

Scottish House Condition Survey Summary Findings 1996, Scottish Homes (Edinburgh 1996).

Urban Heritage Building Maintenance: Foundations, Delft University of Technology (Delft 1999).

Urban Heritage Building Maintenance: Concrete, Delft University of Technology (Delft 1999).

Urban Heritage Building Maintenance: Iron & Steel, Delft University of Technology (Delft 1999).

The Use of Shingles
on Scottish Roofs

H M Colvin (ed), *Building Accounts of King Henry III* (Oxford 1971).

Eric Gee, *A Glossary of Building Terms used in England from the Conquest to circa 1550* (Frome 1984).

R Hauglid, *Laftekunst: Laftehusets Opprinnelse og Eldste Historie* (Oslo 1980).

Timothy Holden, with contributions by Bruce Walker, Stephen Carter, Magnar M Dalland and J Andrew McMullen, *The Archaeology of Scottish Thatch: TAN 13*, Historic Scotland TCRE Division (Edinburgh 1998).

C F Innocent, *The Development of English Building Construction* (Cambridge 1916).

John Henry Parker, *A Glossary of Terms used in Grecian, Roman, Italian and Gothic Architecture* (three volumes) (Oxford 1845-46).

L F Salzman, *Building in England Down to 1540* (Oxford 1952).

John S Scott, *A Dictionary of Building* (Harmondsworth 1964).

John Alexander Smith, 'Notice of the Shingled Roof of the Tower of the Cannongate Tolbooth, Edinburgh' in *Proceedings of the Society of Antiquaries of Scotland* (sessions 1870-71–1871-72), volume ix, part 1 (Edinburgh 1873).

T H Turner and J H Parker, *Domestic Architecture in England* (three volumes (London 1851, 1853, 1859).

Bruce Walker, 'The Use of "Skailie" in Medieval and Post-Medieval Scotland' in *Antiquity*, volume 75 (March 2001).

Bruce Walker and Christopher McGregor, 'The Evidence from Vernacular Building Studies' in Richard Hingley (ed), *Medieval or later Rural Settlement in Scotland: Management and Preservation*, Historic Scotland (Edinburgh 1993).

Bruce Walker, Christopher McGregor and Gregor Stark, *Thatches and Thatching Techniques: TAN 4*, Historic Scotland TCRE Division (Edinburgh 1996).

Bruce Walker, Christopher McGregor and Gregor Stark, *The Hebridean Blackhouse Technical Advice Note 5: A Guide to Materials, Construction and Maintenance* (Historic Scotland, Edinburgh 1996).